CALL ME BLESSED

A

take up & READ

PUBLICATION

Published by The Word Among Us Press
7115 Guilford Drive, Suite 100
Frederick, Maryland 21704
www.wau.org

22 21 20 19 18 1 2 3 4 5

Nihil Obstat: Msgr. Michael Morgan, J.D., J.C.L.
Censor Librorum
October 22, 2018

Imprimatur: +Most Rev. Felipe J. Estevez, S.T.D.
Diocese of St. Augustine
October 22, 2018

Library of Congress Control Number: 2018962998

Editorial Director: Elizabeth Foss
Editors: Emily DeArdo, Katy Greiner, Rosie Hill, and Meg Hunter-Kilmer
Illustration, Cover Art, & Calligraphy: Kristin Foss
Research & Development: Elizabeth Foss and Colleen Connell

ISBN: 978-1-59325-361-5

Made and printed in the United States of America

take up & READ

COMMUNITY

VISIT US

takeupandread.org

BE SOCIAL

Facebook @takeupandread

Instagram @takeupandread

Twitter @totakeupandread

SEND A NOTE

totakeupandread@gmail.com

CONNECT

#TakeUpAndRead

#CallMeBlessedStudy

Begin.

I am about to do a new thing;
now it springs forth, do you not perceive it?
ISAIAH 43:19

START DATE	PLACE
____ | ____ | ____	____________

I'M FEELING

○ *happy*	○ *anxious*	○ *annoyed*	○ *grateful*	○ ________
○ *excited*	○ *upset*	○ *angry*	○ *confused*	○ ________
○ *joyful*	○ *tired*	○ *sad*	○ *calm*	○ ________

Outside my window:

Clothed in:

Pondering:

Listening to:

In my prayers:

Giving thanks for:

My hope for Call Me Blessed:

INTRODUCTION

Between the covers of this book are the stories of nineteen women of the Bible. Each of the women studied here played a part in the gospel story; each one is a piece of how God wants to reveal himself to women today.

The story of each woman from Scripture is a love letter from God to you; these words can bring your soul alive in the Spirit. Take your time, and get to know each woman intimately. Let Scripture change your heart, change your mind, change your life. Let it impact your own story.

Let each story reveal to you the truth of who God is. We live our lives according to what we believe about the nature of God. His nature is revealed in his word. And, as his daughters, we are imbued with his nature. Scripture can show you who you really are. What does that mean as you go about your daily rounds? We've given you room here on these pages to puzzle that out with your pen. And we've offered a little personal insight from the essayists who wrote the devotionals. We each are moved differently, but sometimes when we study together, we look up from the page and the prayer and say, "Really? You too?"

To deepen our understanding of God's vision for women, we look to the teaching of the Church. Woven into our study are the words of Pope St. John Paul II, primarily from his encyclical *Mulieris Dignitatem* (On the Dignity and Vocation of Women). The late Holy Father wrote with tenderness to women, leaving the legacy of a letter that reminds us that in Jesus we are loved, and we are redeemed. As a good father does, the pope calls us to draw near to God and to watch God draw near to us, to see how we were uniquely created in his image to share our feminine genius generously with the world.

Our lives are lived in classrooms and nurseries, in kitchens and conference rooms. For almost all of us, there is a balance between life in the hustle of the world "out there" and the quiet, hidden service inside our homes. It is as holy to serve God in the little ways as it is to be on the mountaintop. And with time, we recognize that it is as easy to recognize the Holy Spirit in the darkness as it is in the moments that shine—sometimes easier. The moments we invest in the study of Scripture help us to see the holy moments in our workaday world. Choose to make those moments frequent and devoted.

Secular society calls to women in myriad ways and tries to impart its vision of femininity to her. That vision is a flat one compared to the vision

God has. You are a beloved daughter of the King—a gentle, humble servant who is a capable and valiant warrior. Know that truth as you take up and read your Bible, eager to see how he calls to you this day.

Elizabeth Foss
Founder, Take Up and Read

You are a beloved daughter of the King—a gentle, humble servant who is a capable and valiant warrior. Know that truth as you take up and read your Bible, eager to see how he calls to you this day.

Intentional Design

Each of our studies is created with unique, intentional design. We want to connect you with the word and keep you connected throughout the day. In this Scripture study, we walk with you through 20 stories from women in the Bible. We encourage *Lectio Divina* (holy reading) for each woman, to shed light on how God works through each of us. As always, fresh layouts, font design, and original artwork ensure that you have the tools to keep him close to your heart, every day.

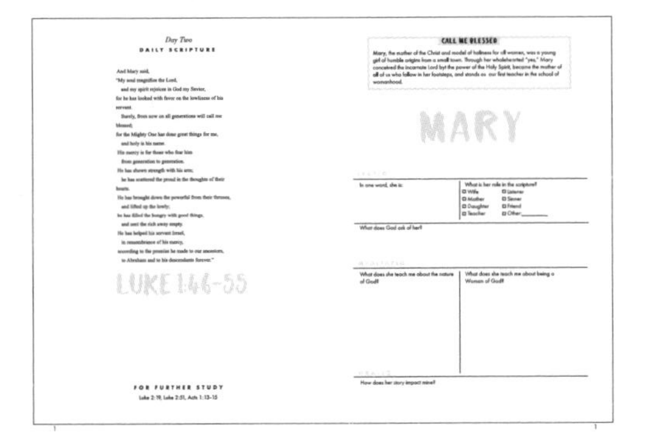

DAILY SCRIPTURE READINGS

This Scripture study includes daily readings and essays to help you intimately get to know these women in the word.

LECTIO DIVINA

Reflect upon the word and make a deep connection with your life by reflection on these components of *Lectio Divina*.

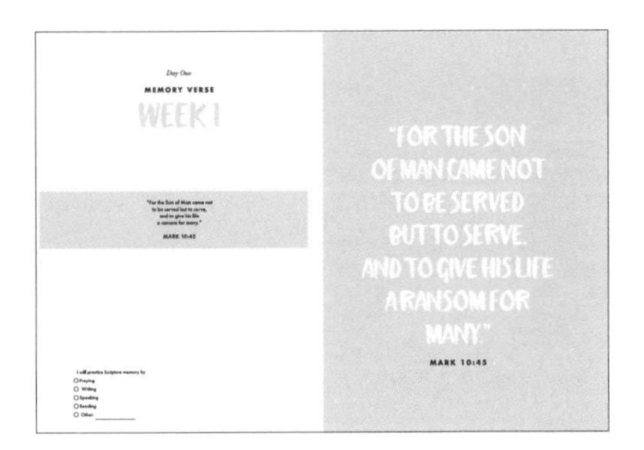

MULIERIS DIGNITATEM

Woven into our study are the words of St. John Paul II, primarily from his encyclical *Mulieris Dignitatem* (On the Dignity and Vocation of Women).

ACTIO

Following the daily essays are *Actio* prompts for you to reflect upon in your heart or to respond directly on the page.

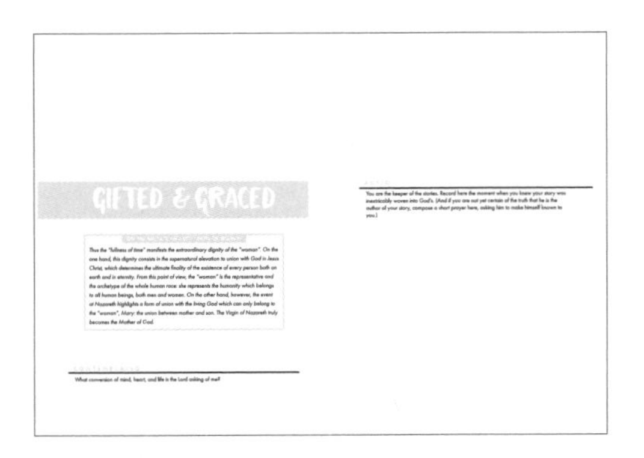

WEEKLY SCRIPTURE VERSE

We will memorize one key verse to reflect upon each week.

At Take Up & Read, we want you to discover what prompts and pages are most useful to your spiritual journey of faith with Christ. There is no perfect way to perform *Lectio Divina*—the important thing is that you take the time to have a conversation with God, using Christ's word as your guide.

Scripture can show you

who you really

are.

Day One

MEMORY VERSE

MARK 10:45

I will practice Scripture memory by

- ◯ Praying
- ◯ Writing
- ◯ Speaking
- ◯ Reading
- ◯ Other: ____________

"FOR THE SON OF MAN CAME NOT TO BE SERVED BUT TO SERVE, AND TO GIVE HIS LIFE A RANSOM FOR MANY."

Day Two

DAILY SCRIPTURE

And Mary said,
"My soul magnifies the Lord,
  and my spirit rejoices in God my Savior,
for he has looked with favor on the lowliness of his servant.
  Surely, from now on all generations will call me blessed;
for the Mighty One has done great things for me,
  and holy is his name.
His mercy is for those who fear him
  from generation to generation.
He has shown strength with his arm;
  he has scattered the proud in the thoughts of their hearts.
He has brought down the powerful from their thrones,
  and lifted up the lowly;
he has filled the hungry with good things,
  and sent the rich away empty.
He has helped his servant Israel,
  in remembrance of his mercy,
according to the promise he made to our ancestors,
  to Abraham and to his descendants forever."

LUKE 1:46-55

FOR FURTHER STUDY

Luke 2:19, 51, Acts 1:13-15

CALL ME BLESSED

Mary, the mother of Christ and model of holiness for all women, was a young girl of humble origins from a small town. Through her wholehearted "yes," Mary conceived the incarnate Lord by the power of the Holy Spirit, became the mother of all of us who follow in her footsteps, and stands as our first teacher in the school of womanhood.

LECTIO

In one word, she is . . .

What is her role in Scripture?

- ☐ Wife
- ☐ Mother
- ☐ Daughter
- ☐ Teacher
- ☐ Listener
- ☐ Sinner
- ☐ Friend
- ☐ Other:__________

What does God ask of her?

MEDITATIO

What does she teach me about the nature of God?

What does she teach me about being a woman of God?

ORATIO

How does her story impact mine?

There is nothing in the Gospel that says she was sweeping, but in my mind, for as long as I can remember, I have imagined that she was sweeping. Most likely, it was an artistic rendering of the Annunciation that first put this idea in my head. Whatever its origin, nothing will shake my sure sense that Mary was sweeping when the angel Gabriel disturbed her work with his grand announcement. And so, every time I sweep (it seems like several dozen times a day), I think about Mary.

If an angel had come to visit me when I was Mary's age, it is highly likely he'd have found me with my nose in a book. I burrowed away for hours most days, hiding from a traumatic childhood and lost in a world of literature where everything (mostly) turned out fine by the end of the story. That sense of narrative was well imbued in me as I entered my adult years. I fully expected that I'd reached the "happily ever after" part as soon as I exchanged wedding vows. What I learned is that actually life is hard, and it tends to offer us one challenge after another—one invitation after another to cooperate with grace to live God's plan, even when it all seems impossible.

Mary knew the story of the Israelites, and she knew all God's promises of a king to come rescue the Hebrew people. She was deeply connected to the story of the God of Israel. But she could not have possibly known her part in the story. She did not know that she was the apex of femininity in God's story of salvation. All she knew was she loved her Lord, and he was asking the impossible of her and promising that it was possible.

She assented to carry the Messiah (see Luke 1:31), not knowing at all how that could come to be, but definitely having some sense of the consequences of being found inexplicably pregnant while betrothed to an esteemed man. For all the Christmas songs and soft oil renderings of Madonna and Child, we know that from the moment she gave her *fiat* to the moment of sorrow at the foot of the cross, Mary lived an incredibly difficult life.

Leaning on a broom and looking in wonder at the angel, she didn't entertain all the ifs, ands, and buts. She did ask how this could be, and when he answered cryptically, she gave her full assent to this astonishing plan, acknowledging only that she was the servant of the Lord. That was enough. Whether sweeping the floor or carrying God in her very person or standing at the foot of a horrific instrument of torture watching her beloved child suffer, she was all in for God.

She was his handmaiden, there by her own assent to serve the Lord with her life.

As my children grow up, one of the most difficult truths I have to impart is the reality that life is hard, that I can't promise that everything is going to be okay—ever—in this world. The hardest moment of parenting might be that moment when I look at a tear-stained face and acknowledge that this is no longer a child who thinks life is a fairy tale, but a young adult with a dawning realization that life is actually a series of challenges that each demands an assent of will and an act of faith. Our children recognize that the world is broken and that they are sons and daughters of Eve.

I can offer them the hope of heaven, but I can't honestly tell them that once they hurdle whatever the present challenge is, life will be easy or even easier than it is right now. I've lived too long, seen too many serious situations arise too often, one right after another, to allow myself to offer that false hope.

Instead, I offer to my children—to the children of Eve—Mary, a humble servant who received our Lord into herself and then spent her lifetime clinging to the promises of God, treasuring them in her heart. She did not know how this story would go; she could not skip to the back of the book and read the ending when the tension in the middle was building unbearably. Instead, she moved from one plot twist to the next, quietly contemplating at every turn (see Luke 2:19, 51).

Mary held the treasure our Lord offered her at the Annunciation in her heart. She was the keeper of the story of Jesus' childhood. She was the one who knew the continuum of his life on earth from beginning to end. And so she stayed with the apostles after he died, and she prayed with them, faithfully imparting the story entrusted to her.

In the nascent Church, she passes on to the disciples her memories of the Incarnation, the infancy, the hidden life, and the mission of her divine Son as a priceless treasure, thus helping to make him known and to strengthen the faith of believers.

> *We have no information about Mary's activity in the early Church, but we may suppose that after Pentecost her life would have continued to be hidden and discreet, watchful and effective. Since she was enlightened and guided by the Spirit, she exercised a deep influence on the community of the Lord's disciples.*
> —Pope St. John Paul II (General Audience, May 28, 1997)

And so, the girl with the broom becomes the mother of the Church—the mother of us all, the keeper of the story, the one who brushes away the hair stuck to our tear-soaked cheeks and acknowledges that all is not a fairy tale here, but that there is more—so much more.

And our stories are just begun.

Elizabeth Foss

GIFTED & GRACED

ON THE DIGNITY AND VOCATION OF WOMEN

Thus the "fullness of time" manifests the extraordinary dignity of the "woman." On the one hand, this dignity consists in the supernatural elevation to union with God in Jesus Christ, which determines the ultimate finality of the existence of every person both on earth and in eternity. From this point of view, the "woman" is the representative and the archetype of the whole human race: she represents the humanity which belongs to all human beings, both men and women. On the other hand, however, the event at Nazareth highlights a form of union with the living God which can only belong to the "woman," Mary: the union between mother and son. The Virgin of Nazareth truly becomes the Mother of God. (4)

CONTEMPLATIO

What conversion of mind, heart, and life is the Lord asking of me?

MULIERIS DIGNITATEM | Woven into our study are the words of Pope St. John Paul II, primarily from his encyclical *Mulieris Dignitatem* (On the Dignity and Vocation of Women). See the introduction on page 6 for more information.

ACTIO

You are the keeper of the stories. Record here the moment when you knew your story was inextricably woven into God's. (And if you are not yet certain of the truth that he is the author of your story, compose a short prayer here, asking him to make himself known to you.)

Day Three

DAILY SCRIPTURE

Mordecai told them to reply to Esther, "Do not think that in the king's palace you will escape any more than all the other Jews. For if you keep silence at such a time as this, relief and deliverance will rise for the Jews from another quarter, but you and your father's family will perish. Who knows? Perhaps you have come to royal dignity for just such a time as this." Then Esther said in reply to Mordecai, "Go, gather all the Jews to be found in Susa, and hold a fast on my behalf, and neither eat nor drink for three days, night or day. I and my maids will also fast as you do. After that I will go to the king, though it is against the law; and if I perish, I perish." Mordecai then went away and did everything as Esther had ordered him.

ESTHER 4:13-17

FOR FURTHER STUDY

Esther 3:1-6; 4; 8:1-7; Hebrews 4:14-16

CALL ME BLESSED

Esther was a young Jewish girl whose family was brought to Persia as captives. After their deaths, she was raised by Mordecai, a cousin, who loved her and cared for her throughout her life. In the Book of Esther, she is brought by force to the palace of King Ahasuerus, who chooses her to be his queen. God's providential action places Esther in the position to use her beauty and strength to liberate the Jewish people and save her nation.

ESTHER

LECTIO

In one word, she is . . .

What is her role in Scripture?

- ☐ Wife
- ☐ Mother
- ☐ Daughter
- ☐ Teacher
- ☐ Listener
- ☐ Sinner
- ☐ Friend
- ☐ Other:__________

What does God ask of her?

MEDITATIO

What does she teach me about the nature of God?

What does she teach me about being a woman of God?

ORATIO

How does her story impact mine?

If the circumstances of her birth tell us anything, Esther was not meant to be a woman of power and influence. She was a poor Jewish girl, a child of captives soon orphaned in a land that was not her own. Raised by a man who was her uncle's son, Esther has very few people left in her life at the time she arrives on the scene of this Old Testament tale of salvation history.

Chance brings Esther to the palace of King Ahasuerus, and her physical beauty garners her attention and favor in the crowd of many women. But it is Esther's courage, wisdom, and steadfastness that win her great influence over the king and his kingdom, allowing her to change the course of history for the Jewish people.

Mordecai, Esther's cousin and formerly her guardian, implores Queen Esther to take the risk required to save the Jewish people from the evil plot of Haman. Knowing she will be risking her own life, he exhorts her to consider that perhaps she has come to this position of power and influence "for just such a time as this," at a moment when she can use that position to save thousands of lives (Esther 4:14). Esther heeds Mordecai's wise words, and the results undeniably mark Jewish history forever.

The words of *Mulieris Dignitatem* ring out a call to us, the women of today, that echo Mordecai's plea to Esther. We have reached an age in which women have a power and influence in our society and culture heretofore unexperienced. And the Church enjoins us to use that influence for the good of our world, to be women "imbued with a spirit of the Gospel" who lift a fallen mankind with Christ-like love and the hope of salvation. But that power and influence are only effective if we choose courageous action on behalf of the gospel. For most of us, that courage will not place us in a life-threatening situation as it did Esther. However, it will likely require that we lay down our lives for others in small ways every day to witness to the goodness of our God right in our own small sphere of influence. We can be women who courageously shine a light into the darkness and create a new culture of love right where we are.

Yesterday was the first major holiday I spent with my boys since my husband and I separated. I woke up feeling a weight in my chest that pleaded with me to hide away from the pain and hurt and stay right where I was. But I prayed and pushed back and pulled myself together despite the despair that nipped at my heels. One small step at a time, I laid down my life for these sweet souls under my roof. There was a trip to the store and fresh flowers on the table, bacon cheeseburgers and watermelon and ice cream sandwiches, water gun wars and naps side by side, and catching fireflies and watching fireworks. And there were boys who smiled with happy contentment and giggled at the memories made. There were hope and joy alive in my home, a burgeoning of gospel good news we all desperately needed.

I may not have the same level of influence that Queen Esther had to change a nation's entire history. But there is a bloodline right under my own roof whose history can be changed by my courage to embrace hope in the darkness. It is a small, quiet laying down of my life for the sake of theirs. Here, in this house, I am queen of the castle, and I will use the power that role gives me to raise up a small nation of gospel warriors, knowing I am here in this place "for just such a time as this."

Colleen Connell

GIFTED & GRACED

ON THE DIGNITY AND VOCATION OF WOMEN

The hour is coming, in fact has come, when the vocation of women is being acknowledged in its fullness, the hour in which women acquire in the world an influence, an effect and a power never hitherto achieved. That is why, at this moment when the human race is undergoing so deep a transformation, women inbuced with a spirit of the Gospel can do so much to aid mankind in not falling. (1)

CONTEMPLATIO

What conversion of mind, heart, and life is the Lord asking of me?

ACTIO

How are you being called to use your influence in the world of your everyday life to aid those around you in accessing God's grace and mercy? From where are you drawing strength to change history as you—and the people you love—make it?

Day Four

DAILY SCRIPTURE

Early on the first day of the week, while it was still dark, Mary Magdalene came to the tomb and saw that the stone had been removed from the tomb. So she ran and went to Simon Peter and the other disciple, the one whom Jesus loved, and said to them, "They have taken the Lord out of the tomb, and we do not know where they have laid him." Then Peter and the other disciple set out and went toward the tomb. The two were running together, but the other disciple outran Peter and reached the tomb first. He bent down to look in and saw the linen wrappings lying there, but he did not go in. Then Simon Peter came, following him, and went into the tomb. He saw the linen wrappings lying there, and the cloth that had been on Jesus' head, not lying with the linen wrappings but rolled up in a place by itself. Then the other disciple, who reached the tomb first, also went in, and he saw and believed; for as yet they did not understand the scripture, that he must rise from the dead. Then the disciples returned to their homes.

But Mary stood weeping outside the tomb. As she wept, she bent over to look into the tomb; and she saw two angels in white, sitting where the body of Jesus had been lying, one at the head and the other at the feet. They said to her, "Woman, why are you weeping?" She said to them, "They have taken away my Lord, and I do not know where they have laid him." When she had said this, she turned around and saw Jesus standing there, but she did not know that it was Jesus. Jesus said to her, "Woman, why are you weeping? Whom are you looking for?" Supposing him to be the gardener, she said to him, "Sir, if you have carried him away, tell me where you have laid him, and I will take him away." Jesus said to her, "Mary!" She turned and said to him in Hebrew, "Rabbouni!" (which means Teacher). Jesus said to her, "Do not hold on to me, because I have not yet ascended to the Father. But go to my brothers and say to them, 'I am ascending to my Father and your Father, to my God and your God.'" Mary Magdalene went and announced to the disciples, "I have seen the Lord"; and she told them that he had said these things to her.

JOHN 20:1-18

FOR FURTHER STUDY

Mark 15:33-47; Luke 8:1-3; 24:1-12; Mark 16:1-11

CALL ME BLESSED

Mary Magdalene is first introduced to us by Luke as a part of the group of female disciples whom Jesus had freed from demonic spirits. As the story of our Lord draws to its climax, Mary Magdalene is ever present. She is one of the few followers left at the foot of the cross at the time of Jesus' death, and she is the one mourning him at the tomb when he appears to announce his resurrection. Jesus sends her to announce the good news, earning her the traditional title "apostle to the Apostles."

MARY MAGDALENE

LECTIO

In one word, she is . . .

What is her role in Scripture?

- ☐ Wife
- ☐ Mother
- ☐ Daughter
- ☐ Teacher
- ☐ Listener
- ☐ Sinner
- ☐ Friend
- ☐ Other:__________

What does God ask of her?

MEDITATIO

What does she teach me about the nature of God?

What does she teach me about being a woman of God?

ORATIO

How does her story impact mine?

One of the beautiful things about Jesus taking on a human nature is that every interaction he has with someone in the Gospels reveals something about how God loves us deeply and personally. In his relationship with Mary Magdalene, he shows us how much he wants to heal us and wants to restore us, not just to him, but also to ourselves.

Mary Magdalene is portrayed in all four Gospels as a loyal and devoted friend. Examples of her devotion are tender and loving: she bathed Jesus' feet with her tears and anointed his feet with costly oil. She waited at the foot of the cross next to his mother, Mary, while most of the other disciples scattered out of fear. She helped prepare his body for burial—something only the closest of friends or family did—and was the first to go to the tomb and find it empty. When she became the first to see the risen Christ, she became, as St. John Paul II writes in *Mulieris Dignitatem*, the "apostle of the Apostles." He adds that "this event, in a sense, crowns all that has been said previously about Christ entrusting divine truths to women as well as men" (16).

But to understand why Mary Magdalene became this devoted and why Christ rewarded her loyalty so uniquely, we need to know the beginning of their story.

The first time she is mentioned in the Bible, she is casually introduced as one of the women who followed Jesus after he had expelled seven demons from her.

Seven.

Stop for a moment, and think of what her waking hours must have felt like before he met her. Anguish? Mental and physical illness? Intense pain and suffering? Very likely, since they are the standard tricks demons have to make humans miserable.

Think about the last time you were in anguish—maybe a relationship was at a breaking point, a financial crisis howled at your door, an injury or illness left you white-knuckling your chair, or grief had its blinding grasp on you. In that pain, having a friend—earthly or heavenly—offer comfort, support, or healing will forge the closest of loyalties. So imagine if that friend took away your pain completely.

Jesus came to Mary Magdalene and healed her. Restored her to herself. It's the very reason why he came into the world—to free us from the tyranny of the devil and to restore humanity to itself and to God. It's God's master plan of love. It plays out in big eschatological ways and also in deeply personal ways.

Her response to this gift from Jesus was an active one, filled with the uniquely feminine qualities of being receptive, generous, and sensitive. She looked for ways for Jesus to feel her love. She followed him everywhere. When she bathed his feet with her tears and anointed him with expensive oil, the other men in the room didn't understand her response or her generosity and ridiculed her for wasting money on the oil. But Jesus and Mary Magdalene were on another plane, living the central Messianic message in that room already: the Savior and the saved.

When he was on the cross, Jesus' mother and Mary Magdalene didn't allow their love to be cast out by fear. The fullness of who they were as women shone in their steadfast sensitivity to Jesus during his passion. And the depth of her love was met with the height of the good news of his resurrection.

In Jesus' encounter with Mary Magdalene, we can see so much about God's relationship with humanity. He wants us to receive his gift of healing and freedom from sin, and when we receive it, we are restored to ourselves and transformed into our truest, fullest selves. For women this includes the fullness of our feminine genius, and we find our hearts tender and open, receptive and generous. These are the very things required for love to take root and grow.

Katie Curtis

GIFTED & GRACED

ON THE DIGNITY AND VOCATION OF WOMEN

Hence she came to be called "the apostle of the Apostles." Mary Magdalene was the first eyewitness of the Risen Christ, and for this reason she was also the first to bear witness to him before the Apostles. This event, in a sense, crowns all that has been said previously about Christ entrusting divine truths to women as well as men. One can say that this fulfilled the words of the Prophet: "I will pour out my spirit on all flesh; your sons and your daughters shall prophesy" (Jl 3:1). On the fiftieth day after Christ's Resurrection, these words are confirmed once more in the Upper Room in Jerusalem, at the descent of the Holy Spirit, the Paraclete (cf. Act 2:17). (16)

CONTEMPLATIO

What conversion of mind, heart, and life is the Lord asking of me?

ACTIO

What are the ways Christ is filling you with "divine truths" to draw you nearer to him while he also sends you out to share the salvation message? How are you making time for those truths to take root in your heart?

Day Five

DAILY SCRIPTURE

Then Jesus, again greatly disturbed, came to the tomb. It was a cave, and a stone was lying against it. Jesus said, "Take away the stone." Martha, the sister of the dead man, said to him, "Lord, already there is a stench because he has been dead four days." Jesus said to her, "Did I not tell you that if you believed, you would see the glory of God?" So they took away the stone. And Jesus looked upward and said, "Father, I thank you for having heard me. I knew that you always hear me, but I have said this for the sake of the crowd standing here, so that they may believe that you sent me." When he had said this, he cried with a loud voice, "Lazarus, come out!" The dead man came out, his hands and feet bound with strips of cloth, and his face wrapped in a cloth. Jesus said to them, "Unbind him, and let him go."

Many of the Jews therefore, who had come with Mary and had seen what Jesus did, believed in him.

JOHN 11:38-45

FOR FURTHER STUDY

John 11:1-45; 12:1-8

CALL ME BLESSED

Mary of Bethany is sister to Jesus' dear friends Martha and Lazarus. In the town of Bethany, just outside of Jerusalem, the family's home is a familiar stopping point for Jesus in the Gospels. Mary is most well-known for her attentive reception of Jesus and his teachings and the vulnerability with which she opened her heart to the Messiah. This faithful friend of Jesus was also a faith-filled woman who believed in his power to save and bring life from death, becoming a prophetic voice of his redemptive action.

MARY OF BETHANY

LECTIO

In one word, she is . . .

What is her role in Scripture?

☐ Wife
☐ Mother
☐ Daughter
☐ Teacher
☐ Listener
☐ Sinner
☐ Friend
☐ Other:__________

What does God ask of her?

MEDITATIO

What does she teach me about the nature of God?

What does she teach me about being a woman of God?

ORATIO

How does her story impact mine?

This isn't an "everything happens for a reason" story. At least, it's not one in which I recognize and share the reason with you.

My father passed away suddenly from a cardiac arrest at age fifty-two. He was a high school English teacher who left for spring break and never came back and left us with no main breadwinner, a wife with four kids aged twelve to twenty-one, a stack of ungraded papers, and a huge well of grief.

In the hospital, we waited for a Lazarus moment. After CPR on the scene didn't restart his heart, four shocks with a defibrillator did, and we had hope. Dad was unconscious due to hypothermic sedation, and we thought that when he "warmed back up," he'd be back. Dad lost consciousness on the feast of St. Joseph while delivering mulch with my brother, and he never regained consciousness, passing away in a nearby hospital while our parish celebrated the Easter Vigil.

He'd proposed to my mom on Holy Saturday twenty-two years earlier. This isn't the place for the full story, but I found Catholic symbolism like that everywhere. Cue my unenthusiastic jazz hands—because it didn't work. The symbolism didn't give way to the miracle. Not for us.

Do I wish my father had been granted a Lazarus miracle? Absolutely. We were all praying for it. His death did not seem to happen for a reason for all of us who prayed so fervently for a miracle. From my vantage point, it did not make us "stronger." When you lose one of your best soldiers, your army isn't better. Perhaps the soldiers are filled with vengeance, but they are no stronger. They are, by definition, weaker through loss.

Nothing has challenged or confirmed my faith more than my father's passing—in fact, because of his death, I am assured that heaven is real, but I couldn't talk to God for months after Dad passed. I wasn't exactly mad at God—which I believe you can be, by the way; his big shoulders can take it. But I couldn't speak to him. For months, I just talked to Dad instead.

My youngest sister said that she's sure that God is real, but she's not sure that she trusts him. Yup, I get that.

What I find most intriguing about the story of Mary of Bethany is the feeling I never got from my own story: an overwhelming sense of divine purpose, the feeling that all of this did happen for a reason. Jesus knows beforehand that Lazarus will die and will rise. When he hears of Lazarus' illness, the Lord says, "This illness does not lead to death; rather it is for God's glory" (John 11:4). Jesus waits for two days and only leaves after receiving the news of Lazarus' death. When he meets Mary and Martha, who both declare that if he had been there, their brother would not have died, Jesus weeps with them, mourns with them, and then goes to raise their brother from the dead.

Why go through all of that? Why challenge their faith; why mourn? It feels, to someone who has lingered at a deathbed, like a trick, like a doctor who had a cure but refused to say so until the last minute.

Jesus did so because with Lazarus, everything did happen for a reason. Life—not death—does indeed happen for a reason. A great, terrible, and glorious reason for the salvation history books.

This is the miracle that sends the Jews to the Pharisees. This is the miracle that pushes them over the edge. Jesus, in giving this man back his life, brings his own death.

When I was a kid, if I took a tumble and scraped my knee, my mom would console me by saying, "I know, I know it hurts, I know." I thought you were supposed to say that when you were hurting, so I'd go up to her, pointing to my wound and saying, "I know, I know, I know" through my tears. And she'd hold me and chorus with me: "I know, I know, I know."

After Dad's passing, if I did think of God, he was saying that. He was crying with me, holding me, saying, "I know, I know it hurts, I know." I was upset that I was hurting, upset he couldn't fix it, and I wanted to go back to the way things were, please. He'd just let me cry. He'd mourn with me, like he did with Mary of Bethany.

I know, I know.

In death, God offers me neither answers nor reasons. But he says, "I know."

Katy Greiner

GIFTED & GRACED

MORE WISDOM FROM ST JOHN PAUL II

Christ responds neither directly nor abstractly to human questioning about the meaning of suffering. Human beings come to know his saving response in so far as they share in the sufferings of Christ. The response which comes from this sharing is before all else a call. It is a vocation. Christ does not explain in some abstract way the reasons for sufferings, but says first of all: "Follow me. Come, with your suffering share in this work of salvation of the world, which is realized through my suffering, by means of my Cross." (Meeting with the Sick and Suffering, January 24, 1998)

CONTEMPLATIO

What conversion of mind, heart, and life is the Lord asking of me?

ACTIO

In what area of your life is a "response of faith" a challenge right now—a place where there is seemingly no reason for what is happening? When your heart cannot resonate with poetic "things of God," what is your response to him, to his love, and to the knowledge that he sees and knows your heart in that moment?

Day Six

DAILY SCRIPTURE

Therefore, I will now allure her,
and bring her into the wilderness,
and speak tenderly to her.
From there I will give her her vineyards,
and make the Valley of Achor a door of hope.
There she shall respond as in the days of her youth,
as at the time when she came out of the land of Egypt.

HOSEA 2:14-15

FOR FURTHER STUDY

Hosea 1:2; Joshua 1:5; Hebrews 13:5; Psalm 23:6; Hosea 2:23

CALL ME BLESSED

Gomer is a woman described as a harlot in the Book of Hosea. Instructed by God, the prophet Hosea takes her as a wife and then watches in anguish as she is unfaithful and wayward. However, Hosea follows God's heart for his people, going after Gomer and purchasing her out of the slavery into which she eventually falls and bringing her home to him. Gomer's life is an unforgettable picture of the mercy of God calling us all back to the safety of his love.

GOMER

LECTIO

In one word, she is . . .

What is her role in Scripture?

- ☐ Wife
- ☐ Mother
- ☐ Daughter
- ☐ Teacher
- ☐ Listener
- ☐ Sinner
- ☐ Friend
- ☐ Other:________

What does God ask of her?

MEDITATIO

What does she teach me about the nature of God?

What does she teach me about being a woman of God?

ORATIO

How does her story impact mine?

I was a teenager when my father left. Desperate to escape an unhappy marriage and a continuing cycle of addiction, he walked out. I understood why he left. I could not wrap my brain around why he didn't take my sister and me with him. I knew how much he loved me, and I couldn't reconcile fatherhood and abandonment. Seven years later, I sat in an empty classroom and talked with a priest about my struggle to see God as a faithful father who would never forsake his child. He suggested that I turn to Hosea and see God as a husband instead.

At the time of this conversation, I had been married only four years; my husband, Mike, and I had welcomed our first child into the world, and we'd walked together through the trial of cancer, chemotherapy, and radiation. Mike never left my side. Instead, he stood in those hardest hours and infused his strength into my whole being. Yes. On that day, in that classroom, I could easily see how God-as-husband would work for me.

What I didn't see coming is that looking at God through the lens of the Book of Hosea meant I was Gomer, the harlot Hosea married, the woman who was his unfaithful wife. To be unfaithful to my husband was unfathomable. I could not imagine being a prostitute or even being adulterous, so this exercise in envisioning God began to short circuit.

No doubt many Christian women have wrestled with finding themselves in Gomer. We can't fathom being a harlot, but God's message here to Israel—and to us—is that everyone who pursues love in unholy places is a prostitute. God made Israel for himself. And he made me (and you) for himself. He wants to tenderly care for and protect me. He wants me to surrender to his embrace, giving myself entirely to the love he pours out unconditionally. I can be faithfully married to the one true God, or I can sell myself for something less. There is no in-between.

I am the woman who has been given God, but I still take my eyes from his face and turn to look at other things—shiny objects of temptation that divert my attention from the life of truth and grace that God has promised to me. I look for love in the affirmation of other women, in the accolades bestowed on my children, in the likes and follows on social media. And it's not just that I have other loves; it's that I fall into other sins and into the despair that is the fruit they bear.

When Israel turned from God repeatedly, distracted by false idols and given to earthly pleasures, the Lord told the prophet Hosea, "Go, take for yourself a wife of whoredom and have children of whoredom, for the land commits great whoredom by forsaking the LORD" (1:2). The marriage of Hosea and Gomer was a parable by which to teach Israel the cycle of sin, even in the presence of God's self-giving love. It was the story God told the Israelites to invite them to understand the nature of his love. Their "love story" tells me that God is the true lover of my soul.

He will never leave me or forsake me (Joshua 1:5; Hebrews 13:5). Further, despite the fact that I sometimes run hard away from him, his goodness and mercy will pursue me all the days of my life (see Psalm 23:6).

God calls us to a love affair with Jesus. We will be disappointed by men on earth—by our fathers, by our husbands, by our sons. And we'll be disappointed by women too. Truth? There is no one on this planet who will love us perfectly.

And so, God calls us to run to him. He wants us to relentlessly pursue a relationship with him. He promises that he is up to the task of perfect love. Truthfully, nothing else will ever fully satisfy me. No one else will totally complete me. I am his girl; he is my God (see Hosea 2:23)—entirely and always.

Elizabeth Foss

GIFTED & GRACED

ON THE DIGNITY AND VOCATION OF WOMEN

These words of Genesis refer directly to marriage, but indirectly they concern the different spheres of social life: the situations in which the woman remains disadvantaged or discriminated against by the fact of being a woman. The revealed truth concerning the creation of the human being as male and female constitutes the principal argument against all the objectively injurious and unjust situations which contain and express the inheritance of the sin which all human beings bear within themselves. The books of Sacred Scripture confirm in various places the actual existence of such situations and at the same time proclaim the need for conversion, that is to say, for purification from evil and liberation from sin: from what offends neighbour, what "diminishes" man, not only the one who is offended but also the one who causes the offence. This is the unchangeable message of the Word revealed by God. In it is expressed the biblical "ethos" until the end of time. (10)

CONTEMPLATIO

What conversion of mind, heart, and life is the Lord asking of me?

ACTIO

Is there an area of your life in which you know in your heart that you have distanced yourself from God? How can recognizing that both the need for conversion and the unfailing mercy of God are universal give you the courage to examine your heart?

SELAH

Use this day for pause, prayer, praise, and rest.

Weekly Check-In

THE BEST TIME TO STUDY	A PLACE I FIND QUIET
______________________	______________________

AS I STUDY *CALL ME BLESSED*, I'M FEELING

○ *happy*	○ *anxious*	○ *annoyed*	○ *grateful*	○ ________
○ *excited*	○ *upset*	○ *angry*	○ *confused*	○ ________
○ *joyful*	○ *tired*	○ *sad*	○ *calm*	○ ________

My heart is changing:

God is changing:

Scripture I can't shake:

A woman of God I want to reflect:

Women in my prayers:

Asking for Mary's intercession:

Grateful for:

Day Eight

MEMORY VERSE

ISAIAH 54:7

I will practice Scripture memory by

- ◯ Praying
- ◯ Writing
- ◯ Speaking
- ◯ Reading
- ◯ Other: ____________

FOR A BRIEF
MOMENT
I ABANDONED YOU,
BUT WITH GREAT
COMPASSION
I WILL GATHER YOU.

Day Nine

DAILY SCRIPTURE

But Ruth said,
"Do not press me to leave you
or to turn back from following you!
Where you go, I will go;
where you lodge, I will lodge;
your people shall be my people,
and your God my God.
Where you die, I will die—
there will I be buried.
May the LORD do thus and so to me,
and more as well,
if even death parts me from you!"

RUTH 1:16-17

...But Boaz answered her, "All that you have done for your mother-in-law since the death of your husband has been fully told me, and how you left your father and mother and your native land and came to a people that you did not know before. May the LORD reward you for your deeds, and may you have a full reward from the LORD, the God of Israel, under whose wings you have come for refuge!"

RUTH 2:11-12

FOR FURTHER STUDY

Really, just read all of Ruth. It's not very long and well worth the time.

CALL ME BLESSED

Ruth was a Moabite woman who married a Hebrew man whose family migrated to Moabite territory to seek relief from famine. Ruth's husband, his brother, and his father died in close succession, leaving Ruth, her sister-in-law, and her mother-in-law, Naomi, bereft and at risk of living in great poverty. When Naomi offered Ruth the freedom to remain in her own nation rather than follow Naomi back to her homeland, Ruth chose faithfulness to Naomi instead of her kinsmen and in Israel wed Boaz and bore a son whose lineage leads straight to King David.

RUTH

LECTIO

In one word, she is . . .

What is her role in Scripture?

- ☐ Wife
- ☐ Mother
- ☐ Daughter
- ☐ Teacher
- ☐ Listener
- ☐ Sinner
- ☐ Friend
- ☐ Other:__________

What does God ask of her?

MEDITATIO

What does she teach me about the nature of God?

What does she teach me about being a woman of God?

ORATIO

How does her story impact mine?

"… because the hand of the LORD has turned against me." (Ruth 1:13)

Loss is hard.

After she loses her two sons and husband, Naomi sends her daughter-in-law Ruth away, asking her to return to her own people. Orpah, the other son's widow, heads back to her home in tears. Ruth has a decision to make. Will she stay with the bitter mother-in-law who asked her to leave? Or will she return home, forget about Naomi, and find a new husband? It's a complicated choice, but without hesitation, she stays with Naomi and devotes her life to living like her mother-in-law.

Considering the time period, Ruth's best interest would have been to go home and remarry. In ancient Moab, a widowed young woman with no men left in the family was not advised to remain single. Who would take care of Ruth, now that she had no husband? How much time did she have left in her lifetime to find a new husband and to have children? What skills did Ruth possess to take care of herself? How would she take care of Naomi?

This decision is major, not only to Ruth and Naomi, but to salvation history. This is the moment that paves the way for the birth of David's grandfather, which leads us to David and, ultimately, much later, to Jesus. The moment of Ruth's decision connects the Old Testament to the New Testament. This is a moment of God's promise. Ruth's role is pivotal to our Christian faith and culture.

Have you ever witnessed a loved one struggling, at a very low point? Maybe she has lost her husband and two sons, or maybe it was something as common as a really, really bad day? She falls victim to her current fate. She blames God. She isolates herself. She claims a new identity as a bitter woman. What is your role in her pain? Do you walk away and let her struggle alone? Or do you stay and defend her? Even in her own mourning, Ruth stays to defend Naomi's legacy.

Ruth keeps it very simple. She plans to live like Naomi—worship, sleep, and die like Naomi. Her actions are everything. Her pain and anxieties are pushed aside. There is no written record of them. By her actions, we can assume that, like Mary, Ruth is characterized by her faithfulness and her obedience to God. She, too, says an important and historic "yes" to the Lord.

We live in a throwaway culture, in which everything is seen as temporary and replaceable. For some, even people are disposable—forgotten friends, neglected relationships with difficult people, and abandoned family. We forget that in God's kingdom, there is no small role. While there's not always a time and place to be a Ruth for each Naomi, there is a time and place to keep those people in our prayers, commending them directly to our Lord.

When we surrender in love, we ignite a powerful force that can change the world. Ruth seems to intuit how best to serve in her situation. She becomes an instrument in the plan for redemption and salvation—all because she stays.

Faith grants grace. When we live our faith, we live in grace. But acting in faith takes vulnerability. It's okay to be the gift someone else needs. It's okay to step out of your comfort zone and follow a hurt woman, in the name of God.

In our time, defending a hurt woman can look radical, like Ruth's role, or it can be simple. Check in even when she doesn't reach out. Show up with dinner at the door. Leave it on the porch. Text when she doesn't respond. Call when she doesn't answer. Remember that Christ's kingdom is endless and that each "yes" is important. Ruth chose to stay, and the prophecy began to bloom.

Kristin Foss

GIFTED & GRACED

ON THE DIGNITY AND VOCATION OF WOMEN

Being a person means striving towards self-realization (the Council speaks of self-discovery), which can only be achieved "through a sincere gift of self." The model for this interpretation of the person is God himself as Trinity, as a communion of Persons. To say that man is created in the image and likeness of God means that man is called to exist "for" others, to become a gift. (7)

CONTEMPLATIO

What conversion of mind, heart, and life is the Lord asking of me?

ACTIO

You were created to know, love, and serve God. You love and serve God when you love and serve other people. Further, you will discover who you truly are—who you were created to be—when you give yourself away in the service to others. Right now, where are your opportunities to give?

Day Ten

DAILY SCRIPTURE

But Naomi said, "Turn back, my daughters, why will you go with me? Do I still have sons in my womb that they may become your husbands? Turn back, my daughters, go your way, for I am too old to have a husband. Even if I thought there was hope for me, even if I should have a husband tonight and bear sons, would you then wait until they were grown? Would you then refrain from marrying? No, my daughters, it has been far more bitter for me than for you, because the hand of the LORD has turned against me."

FOR FURTHER STUDY

Ruth 1:19-21

CALL ME BLESSED

Naomi's story is intimately linked to Ruth's, the focus of yesterday's reflection. Naomi became a widow and childless mother while living in a foreign land. All she had left were her two daughters-in-law and the hope of returning to her homeland. She risked ending up completely alone when she gave her daughters-in-law the choice to stay with their families. Ruth's choice to stay at Naomi's side gives Naomi hope and new life, and she becomes the impetus behind Ruth's union with Boaz, affecting the course of salvation history.

NAOMI

LECTIO

In one word, she is . . .

What is her role in Scripture?

- ☐ Wife
- ☐ Mother
- ☐ Daughter
- ☐ Teacher
- ☐ Listener
- ☐ Sinner
- ☐ Friend
- ☐ Other:__________

What does God ask of her?

MEDITATIO

What does she teach me about the nature of God?

What does she teach me about being a woman of God?

ORATIO

How does her story impact mine?

I think that mothers-in-law get a bad rap. Much maligned in popular culture, it is almost universally assumed that the mother-in-law's relationship with her daughter-in-law will be prickly. The reality is that when a woman has invested a lifetime in raising a son, it's never going to be a simple thing to let that "child" go, no matter who is at the ready to be the grown boy's wife. Most women truly believe that it is a great joy to see one's children well married. It's just that folding another adult into the life of a family can be challenging when so many pieces of said life are shifting. So if you are a daughter-in-law who wonders about the relationship with your husband's mother, consider the possibility that it's not you. It's her.

Becoming a mother-in-law coincides with midlife. Very few people write about midlife mothering because no one wants to discourage younger women, and no one wants to tell the stories that belong to grown and nearly grown children—stories that frequently break a mother's heart but that are reserved for the privacy of a family. But women at midlife who let down their guard and confide in one another find that they share common threads of unexpected sorrow.

The middle-aged woman who has finally grown into herself as a mother comes to a new stage of life. Her children—now grown—are establishing their own sense of self, often rejecting bits of their childhood in the process, possibly bits that were cherished and chosen by their mother. At the same time, her own parents are failing in health and so are unable to maintain a supportive role and indeed require a great deal of care. And then there is the dying. This is the season when the generation before her dies, leaving a woman to face both the pain of loss and the reality of her own mortality. The ground shifts beneath her feet, and she understands just how little life is under her control. It's not the best time to start a new lifelong relationship. Or is it?

In Naomi's case, all of these midlife challenges were nothing compared to the losses of her sons and husband. Tragedy had stolen from her all that she had and also all that she was. No longer was she a wife and mother. She came to the middle of her life, and upon honestly evaluating it, she told her friends, "Call me no longer Naomi, / call me Mara, / for the Almighty has dealt bitterly with me. / I went away full, / but the LORD has brought me back empty" (Ruth 1:20-21). She believes God is sovereign, but she doesn't believe he is good—at least not for her. So much has spun out of her control that she has no vision for beauty from ashes at the hands of a good God. Instead, she claims bitterness and uses it to identify herself.

Naomi cannot see the gift in front of her. In her grief and her fear, she misses the fact that Ruth stands before her, ready to be "all in" for her and with her, and she tries to send Ruth away from her. What she doesn't recognize is that God has a plan for the rest of her life, it's better than any plan Naomi can imagine, and Ruth is integral to that plan. But first, she has to surrender to his will and accept the friendship and the loyalty of her daughter-in-law.

Ruth proves to be the way forward for Naomi. Sometimes we don't trust that someone truly can be entirely for us, that something new amidst so much sorrow can be a good thing. Sometimes we don't even trust that Jesus is entirely for us. Naomi is the icon—the extreme, instructive rendering—of the primary lesson of midlife: very little is under one's control, but when we learn to surrender, we also let bitterness give way to pleasantness (the meaning of "Naomi" in Hebrew).

I've certainly had my own Naomi moments. I've pushed away the girl who would be my daughter-in-law, and I've tried to reject the unfolding plan for good in the life of my family because I failed to recognize it as God's plan. I imagine God smiling a twinkling smile as I write those words in this book. He knew what I could never have conceived.

The book you hold in your hands now was designed by the "Ruth" in my life. She is happily married to my son, and she is a wonderful mother to my grandchildren. But in the "Wait! There's more!" department, we also work together every day as a team. In the process, we share the joys and sorrows of our respective stations in life. She is my dearest friend, and she is an integral part of the story of renewed hope at midlife.

Don't let the hard knocks in life make you bitter. Don't be afraid. There is someone God intends for good in your life. Open your heart to her. Let her—and God—surprise you for the good.

Elizabeth Foss

GIFTED & GRACED

ON THE DIGNITY AND VOCATION OF WOMEN

Being a person in the image and likeness of God thus also involves existing in a relationship, in relation to the other "I." This is a prelude to the definitive self-revelation of the Triune God: a living unity in the communion of the Father, Son and Holy Spirit. (7)

CONTEMPLATIO

What conversion of mind, heart, and life is the Lord asking of me?

ACTIO

What relationship in your life is God using to surprise you right now? How might the depth of that relationship be enhanced by going "all in" and believing the other person is "all in" for you too?

Day Eleven

DAILY SCRIPTURE

A Samaritan woman came to draw water, and Jesus said to her, “Give me a drink.” (His disciples had gone to the city to buy food.) The Samaritan woman said to him, “How is it that you, a Jew, ask a drink of me, a woman of Samaria?” (Jews do not share things in common with Samaritans.) Jesus answered her, “If you knew the gift of God, and who it is that is saying to you, ‘Give me a drink,’ you would have asked him, and he would have given you living water.” The woman said to him, “Sir, you have no bucket, and the well is deep. Where do you get that living water? Are you greater than our ancestor Jacob, who gave us the well, and with his sons and his flocks drank from it?” Jesus said to her, “Everyone who drinks of this water will be thirsty again, but those who drink of the water that I will give them will never be thirsty. The water that I will give will become in them a spring of water gushing up to eternal life.” The woman said to him, “Sir, give me this water, so that I may never be thirsty or have to keep coming here to draw water.”

Jesus said to her, “Go, call your husband, and come back.” The woman answered him, “I have no husband.” Jesus said to her, “You are right in saying, ‘I have no husband’; for you have had five husbands, and the one you have now is not your husband. What you have said is true!” The woman said to him, “Sir, I see that you are a prophet. Our ancestors worshiped on this mountain, but you say that the place where people must worship is in Jerusalem.” Jesus said to her, “Woman, believe me, the hour is coming when you will worship the Father neither on this mountain nor in Jerusalem. You worship what you do not know; we worship what we know, for salvation is from the Jews. But the hour is coming, and is now here, when the true worshipers will worship the Father in spirit and truth, for the Father seeks such as these to worship him. God is spirit, and those who worship him must worship in spirit and truth.” The woman said to him, “I know that Messiah is coming” (who is called Christ). “When he comes, he will proclaim all things to us.” Jesus said to her, “I am he, the one who is speaking to you.”

JOHN 4:7-26

FOR FURTHER STUDY

Please read all of John 4; Matthew 10:42

CALL ME BLESSED

The woman at the well is a story of great impact that shows us just how far Jesus crossed cultural boundaries to reach the hearts of women. The woman was a Samaritan, an unclean pagan with whom a Jew would not interact and a woman whose long string of marriages had earned her quite the reputation. She reacts with surprise and even a hint of bitterness when Jesus first offers her the gift of life-giving water. But her later acceptance of Jesus' message and mercy becomes one of the greatest examples of conversion of heart in the New Testament.

WOMAN AT THE WELL

LECTIO

In one word, she is . . .

What is her role in Scripture?

☐ Wife ☐ Listener
☐ Mother ☐ Sinner
☐ Daughter ☐ Friend
☐ Teacher ☐ Other:__________

What does God ask of her?

MEDITATIO

What does she teach me about the nature of God?

What does she teach me about being a woman of God?

ORATIO

How does her story impact mine?

She'd been married five times, and the man she had now was not her husband. This woman had not had an easy life. Maybe she'd buried five husbands, or maybe she'd been divorced five times. She may have been a victim, or she may have been profoundly guilty. The fact that she was drawing water in the heat of the day certainly implies that she was an outcast, preferring to suffer under the noonday sun rather than enduring the wagging tongues and sidelong glances of the women who gathered at the well in the cool of the evening or in the early morning. The portrait painted by John depicts a broken, bitter, and lonely woman.

Her reaction to Jesus only strengthens that impression. When asked for a drink, she snapped. Then she argued. When she finally opened up, he brought her walls right back up by asking her to call her husband. "I don't have a husband," she muttered. Maybe it's my own decade and a half of singleness that makes me read this with bitterness, but her words seem to be filled with the same pain felt by so many single, divorced, and widowed women down through the centuries. She had thought that this once she could forget her reputation, forget her past. But this man, it seems, was no different from everyone else.

Still, she didn't walk away. When he read her soul and told her that he knew about her previous marriages, about her current partner, she didn't walk away.

Because he didn't walk away.

Jesus had come to Samaria specifically to seek her. When John tells us that "he had to go through Samaria," it's not exactly true (John 4:4). Not in the geographical sense, anyway. He had to pass through Samaria not because the roads demanded it but because there was one woman he had to speak to. One woman he had to love.

He came to the well in the middle of the day because he was looking for her. Not just for any woman, but for this one, the one whose brokenness drew her there. He asked her for a drink, not because he couldn't get one himself, but because he wanted to speak to her. He chose to need her so that he could offer himself to her.

And then he brought the most painful parts of her life into the light. He saw her shame and looked right past it into her heart, loving her all the more because of the things she hated most about herself.

It changed her. She left her water jar behind, abandoning her previous purpose to go back to the very people who had made her life hell and offer them the living water he had given her. Her brokenness brought her to Jesus and, through her, many others. There, on the other side of brokenness, she was a witness, an evangelist.

Like the woman at the well, you may have suffered. You may have sinned or been sinned against, made irrevocably bad decisions and found yourself ostracized because of them. Please know this: you are seen and loved exactly as you are. The God who rose with jagged wounds on his hands and feet can glorify your suffering and make you whole in ways you can only imagine, with scars that give glory to his name.

If your heart has been broken, praise the Lord: it's through broken hearts that grace enters in. Your pain will not be wasted. There will come a day, either here or hereafter, when you will stand with the woman at the well, looking back at a life full of misery with joy instead of shame. You will see how his grace was at work, how your brokenness brought you to him, and you will rejoice.

Jesus is seeking you just as he sought her. Bring him your brokenness, and let him love you just as you are.

Meg Hunter-Kilmer

GIFTED & GRACED

ON THE DIGNITY AND VOCATION OF WOMEN

It is universally admitted—even by people with a critical attitude towards the Christian message—that in the eyes of his contemporaries Christ became a promoter of women's true dignity and of the vocation corresponding to this dignity. At times this caused wonder, surprise, often to the point of scandal: "They marveled that he was talking with a woman" (John 4:27), because this behavior differed from that of his contemporarie. . . .

Christ's way of acting, the Gospel of his words and deeds, is a consistent protest against whatever offends the dignity of women. Consequently, the women who are close to Christ discover themselves in the truth which he "teaches" and "does," even when this truth concerns their "sinfulness." They feel "liberated" by this truth, restored to themselves: they feel loved with "eternal love," with a love which finds direct expression in Christ himself. (12)

CONTEMPLATIO

What conversion of mind, heart, and life is the Lord asking of me?

ACTIO

In what area of life could Christ's love liberate you from seeing yourself as a shameful scandal and instead allow you to embrace the dignity of who you really are in God?

Day Twelve

DAILY SCRIPTURE

Jesus left that place and went away to the district of Tyre and Sidon. Just then a Canaanite woman from that region came out and started shouting, "Have mercy on me, Lord, Son of David; my daughter is tormented by a demon." But he did not answer her at all. And his disciples came and urged him, saying, "Send her away, for she keeps shouting after us." He answered, "I was sent only to the lost sheep of the house of Israel." But she came and knelt before him, saying, "Lord, help me." He answered, "It is not fair to take the children's food and throw it to the dogs." She said, "Yes, Lord, yet even the dogs eat the crumbs that fall from their masters' table." Then Jesus answered her, "Woman, great is your faith! Let it be done for you as you wish." And her daughter was healed instantly.

MATTHEW 15:21-28

FOR FURTHER STUDY

Mark 7:24-30

CALL ME BLESSED

The Canaanite woman is another woman who culturally should not have had access to Jesus. She appears at a moment when Jesus and the disciples are retiring from the building tensions in Jerusalem, looking for rest. The odd tensions in the story can be off-putting at first. But this is a story of a woman of great faith who sees the truth: that Jesus is inviting her to believe and profess that belief more ardently. Jesus uses her insistent faith to poignantly show his disciples that his mercy is for everyone.

THE CANAANITE WOMAN

LECTIO

In one word, she is . . .

What is her role in Scripture?

- ☐ Wife
- ☐ Mother
- ☐ Daughter
- ☐ Teacher
- ☐ Listener
- ☐ Sinner
- ☐ Friend
- ☐ Other:__________

What does God ask of her?

MEDITATIO

What does she teach me about the nature of God?

What does she teach me about being a woman of God?

ORATIO

How does her story impact mine?

The story of the Canaanite woman is my story, the story of a woman whose heart is breaking as she watches her child suffer. This passage, although uncomfortable to read, packs a soul punch that has never left me. I know this woman's heart and recognize that her determination and persistence make her not only a true heroine of the Bible but a true representation of who we are as women in Christ.

When she encounters the apostles, she knows she doesn't belong. She's a different race and religion, and she's mistrusted by everyone there. Yet when everyone tells her to get out and go home, she stays because she knows only Jesus can help her.

After her first request, Jesus is silent. That silence is the hardest for many of us to sit with in our own faith journey. We want a quick answer, to fix it and move on. But imagine with me for a moment what the woman heard in that silence.

Jesus did not say "no." He simply made her wait.

Her next plea is the one that always breaks me when I read it because I, too, have said the same millions of times.

"Lord, help me" (Matthew 15:25).

Jesus does something here that took me years to unpack. He tests her resolve. He tells her that he is here only for the people of Israel, and she is not one of them. At this point, had I been that woman, I might actually have punched him. Obviously, the Lord is still working on me.

But my Canaanite sister has some serious chutzpah. She will not leave, even as the apostles complain. Jesus tosses out a comment equating her with a dog, which in ancient times was the most horrendous of insults, and my girl stays in the fight. When she says, "Yes, Lord, yet even the dogs eat the crumbs that fall from their masters' table," she gives one of the most desperate retorts in the Bible, showing us that her feelings don't matter in this equation (Matthew 15:27). All that matters to her is that her daughter is healed.

In this moment everything changes. Jesus delights in her perseverance, in her bold and striking public profession of faith. When he says, "Woman, great is your faith," he answers her prayer and sends her home to be with her daughter, who is now healed.

He knew what she would say. He knew her heart before she knew her heart. He knew how bold her faith was, but he needed her to know how bold her faith was. He delighted in her persistence, dignity, and strength.

She was a woman who refused to back down when she knew that God was God, and she was not.

My story looks a little different. I, too, begged for my daughter Courtney's life, for her complete restoration and healing from the daily grand mal seizures that racked her brain and crippled her body. I pleaded with God every single day for twenty-two years.

I was consumed with this prayer and refused to turn away from God, even in the silence and the waiting. Like the Canaanite woman, I know who God is, and I was persistent in my pleas. There was no way I was giving up on Courtney, no matter the personal cost to me. God was just going to have to deal with this brash, mouthy, and assertive mother.

In my own life, I faced many obstacles along the way, including times when the people I trusted told me my prayers were useless because God had said "no." My favorite was when they told me that Courtney's condition was due to my own sin. Luckily for my daughter, I was never a woman to take "no" for an answer. Ask my mother.

Looking back now, I can see that all along God had a plan for my daughter's life that was bigger and bolder than I could have imagined. God provided the courage, the grace, and the strength exactly when they were needed to meet the many challenges. He stretched my capacity to love and serve my daughter beyond anything I thought was possible. Most importantly, when it came time for Courtney's healing to come with her death, he offered me comfort. Her suffering was ended even as my own heart was broken. Some may say I didn't get my miracle like the Canaanite woman did for her daughter. I could not disagree more.

The Canaanite woman taught me to persevere in prayer and lay everything out before the Lord. As women of faith, we have to trust that God's plan is exactly what it needs to be for our salvation and for those whom we love. Even if that plan includes scraps from the table.

Mary Lenaburg

GIFTED & GRACED

ON THE DIGNITY AND VOCATION OF WOMEN

Christ speaks to women about the things of God, and they understand them; there is a true resonance of mind and heart, a response of faith. Jesus expresses appreciation and admiration for this distinctly "feminine" response, as in the case of the Canaanite woman (cf. Mt. 15:28). Sometimes he presents this lively faith, filled with love, as an example. He teaches, therefore, taking as his starting-point this feminine response of mind and heart. (15)

CONTEMPLATIO

What conversion of mind, heart, and life is the Lord asking of me?

ACTIO

If you take the faith of the Canaanite woman as your starting place, what do you ask of God today?

Day Thirteen

DAILY SCRIPTURE

One day Elisha was passing through Shunem, where a wealthy woman lived, who urged him to have a meal. So whenever he passed that way, he would stop there for a meal. She said to her husband, "Look, I am sure that this man who regularly passes our way is a holy man of God. Let us make a small roof chamber with walls, and put there for him a bed, a table, a chair, and a lamp, so that he can stay there whenever he comes to us."

One day when he came there, he went up to the chamber and lay down there. He said to his servant Gehazi, "Call the Shunammite woman." When he had called her, she stood before him. He said to him, "Say to her, Since you have taken all this trouble for us, what may be done for you? Would you have a word spoken on your behalf to the king or to the commander of the army?" She answered, "I live among my own people." He said, "What then may be done for her?" Gehazi answered, "Well, she has no son, and her husband is old." He said, "Call her." When he had called her, she stood at the door. He said, "At this season, in due time, you shall embrace a son." She replied, "No, my lord, O man of God; do not deceive your servant."

The woman conceived and bore a son at that season, in due time, as Elisha had declared to her.

2 KINGS 4:8-17

Let mutual love continue. Do not neglect to show hospitality to strangers, for by doing that some have entertained angels without knowing it.

HEBREWS 13:1-2

FOR FURTHER STUDY

Please read all of 2 Kings 4; 8:1-6; 1 Corinthians 11:1-34; Acts 2:11

CALL ME BLESSED

The woman of Shunem is a called "a great woman" in Scripture (2 Kings 4:8, KJV). Shunem was a small farming village in the extended territory where the prophet Elisha ministered. Her story is one of holy hospitality, friendship, and pain. This woman of Shunem placed her trust in God's servant and thus in God, no matter her circumstances. She reveals to us the intimacy with which we are known by God and the lengths to which he will go to draw us near to him.

WOMAN OF SHUNEM

LECTIO

In one word, she is . . .

What is her role in Scripture?

☐ Wife ☐ Listener
☐ Mother ☐ Sinner
☐ Daughter ☐ Friend
☐ Teacher ☐ Other:__________

What does God ask of her?

MEDITATIO

What does she teach me about the nature of God?

What does she teach me about being a woman of God?

ORATIO

How does her story impact mine?

I live in a rather large house. With nine children, we have filled it well. For years, each bedroom was doubled or tripled in order to be home to our children. As they began to leave for homes of their own, one of those rooms became a "guest room." Ah! The glorious luxury that is a guest room! I truly felt like a woman of wealth when I was able to set a room aside just for people who might be passing through and need a room for rest. It was a joy to consider every detail of that room from the perspective of guests who would stay there—art and linens and even a little card with the wifi access code were woven together to provide a place of respite. After a long time of wishing it were so, I felt as if I could at last extend a lavish gesture of hospitality.

The Shunammite woman was a woman of means and social stature who personified the hospitality of the gospel. She knew that she had been given plenty and more, and she understood that with that plenty came the charism of making others welcome. With kindness and care, she anticipated Elisha's need as the missionary journey became more difficult for him, and she prepared a place for him. I'm drawn to this woman because of her hospitality; I want that to be the lesson she holds for me. I can be a holy woman if I take my extra room and "make a small roof chamber with walls, and put there for him a bed, a table, a chair, and a lamp, so that he can stay there whenever he comes" (2 Kings 4:10). This path to holiness is appealing; I like to fluff pillows and make meals.

But that is not where the Lord leaves me. In return for her hospitality, the prophet promised the barren woman a child, and God made good on the promise. She and her husband were delighted by their son, and all was well under their roof. When her son died on her lap, the woman's faith was tested. It is in her grief that she shows us how deep and true her holiness ran. Her first instinct was to run to the holy man of God. When she got there, she was composed when Elisha's servant came to greet her. He asked, "Is it well with the child?" (2 Kings 4:26, RSV).

The child had just died! *No, it's not well. It's not well at all. My heart is shattered into a million pieces, and my grief is unlike anything I've ever felt.*

That's the answer we expect. Instead, his mother answered, "It is well." In that moment, she expressed an unwavering faith in God's ability to heal. Even in the face of death, even though she had just lost the greatest treasure in the world, she said, "It is well." She believed in God's infinite power to make all things well.

She had come alone with only the servant to drive her, a strong woman with strong faith who was determined to seek God's mercy. When she finally saw Elisha, she broke, and our Lord, in his goodness, lets us see that even strong, faithful women feel strong emotions; even they can fall apart, even if just a little bit. I stop here and shake my head in wonder.

I am a strong woman of strong faith. I have opened my home in hospitality and wanted nothing more than a gracious loveliness for the people who visit me there, as well as for my family because of their presence. But I am also a woman who understands in a very personal way that to invite others into our homes—and our hearts—makes us vulnerable to pain as well as to blessing. This path to holiness is a much more treacherous one.

God meets me there. He shows me the unmistakable lesson of the Shunammite woman. She opened her heart with kindness and goodness—graciously bestowing blessing on others. And when her joy turned to sorrow, the Shunammite woman didn't raise her fist to God and ask him why her "reward" was pain. She persevered in faith, bearing witness to the truth that ultimately, God would restore her joy.

Has your joy been shadowed? Has your heart been shattered because you opened it to a stranger? God is in those moments. He perseveres with you. You can believe it will be well.

Elizabeth Foss

GIFTED & GRACED

ON THE DIGNITY AND VOCATION OF WOMEN

"To prophesy" means to express by one's words and one's life "the mighty works of God" (Acts 2:11), preserving the truth and originality of each person, whether woman or man. Gospel "equality," the "equality" of women and men in regard to the "mighty works of God"—manifested so clearly in the words and deeds of Jesus of Nazareth —constitutes the most obvious basis for the dignity and vocation of women in the Church and in the world. Every vocation has a profoundly personal and prophetic meaning. In "vocation" understood in this way, what is personally feminine reaches a new dimension: the dimension of the "mighty works of God," of which the woman becomes the living subject and an irreplaceable witness. (16)

CONTEMPLATIO

What conversion of mind, heart, and life is the Lord asking of me?

ACTIO

Who needs to find a welcome place in your heart right now or needs you to open a safe space for him or her? Where might you become the landing pad for and prophetic witness of the "mighty works of God" (Acts 2:11)?

SELAH

Use this day for pause, prayer, praise, and rest.

Weekly Check-In

THE BEST TIME TO STUDY	A PLACE I FIND QUIET
______________________	______________________

AS I STUDY *CALL ME BLESSED*, I'M FEELING

- ○ *happy* ○ *anxious* ○ *annoyed* ○ *grateful* ○ ____________
- ○ *excited* ○ *upset* ○ *angry* ○ *confused* ○ ____________
- ○ *joyful* ○ *tired* ○ *sad* ○ *calm* ○ ____________

My heart is changing:

God is changing:

Scripture I can't shake:

A woman of God I want to reflect:

Women in my prayers:

Asking for Mary's intercession:

Grateful for:

Day Fifteen

MEMORY VERSE

2 TIMOTHY 1:5

I will practice Scripture memory by

- ◯ Praying
- ◯ Writing
- ◯ Speaking
- ◯ Reading
- ◯ Other: ______________

I AM REMINDED OF
YOUR SINCERE FAITH,
A FAITH THAT LIVED
FIRST IN YOUR
GRANDMOTHER LOIS
AND YOUR MOTHER
EUNICE
AND NOW,
I AM SURE,
LIVES IN YOU.

Day Sixteen

DAILY SCRIPTURE

The name of Amram's wife was Jochebed daughter of Levi, who was born to Levi in Egypt; and she bore to Amram: Aaron, Moses, and their sister Miriam.

NUMBERS 26:59

Now a man from the house of Levi went and married a Levite woman. The woman conceived and bore a son; and when she saw that he was a fine baby, she hid him three months. When she could hide him no longer she got a papyrus basket for him, and plastered it with bitumen and pitch; she put the child in it and placed it among the reeds on the bank of the river. His sister stood at a distance, to see what would happen to him.

The daughter of Pharaoh came down to bathe at the river, while her attendants walked beside the river. She saw the basket among the reeds and sent her maid to bring it. When she opened it, she saw the child. He was crying, and she took pity on him. "This must be one of the Hebrews' children," she said. Then his sister said to Pharaoh's daughter, "Shall I go and get you a nurse from the Hebrew women to nurse the child for you?" Pharaoh's daughter said to her, "Yes." So the girl went and called the child's mother. Pharaoh's daughter said to her, "Take this child and nurse it for me, and I will give you your wages." So the woman took the child and nursed it. When the child grew up, she brought him to Pharaoh's daughter, and she took him as her son. She named him Moses, "because," she said, "I drew him out of the water."

EXODUS 2:1-10

FOR FURTHER STUDY

Exodus 1:1-22; Luke 11:13

CALL ME BLESSED

Jochabed was a faithful Hebrew woman, married to Amram. They were the parents of three children whose stories are told in the book of Exodus: Miriam, Aaron, and Moses. Jochabed's place in salvation history and her renowned courage are centered on the fact that Moses was born during the reign of a pharaoh, probably Rameses II, who, in order to protect his power, sought to ensure that no male Hebrew child born during that time lived. Jochabed's plan to save Moses is the first stage of an epic tale of God's glory revealed.

JOCHABED

LECTIO

In one word, she is . . .

What is her role in Scripture?

☐ Wife ☐ Listener
☐ Mother ☐ Sinner
☐ Daughter ☐ Friend
☐ Teacher ☐ Other:__________

What does God ask of her?

MEDITATIO

What does she teach me about the nature of God?

What does she teach me about being a woman of God?

ORATIO

How does her story impact mine?

I took my child to college yesterday. I drove him two hours from home, helped him unpack his clothes, sat with him and tried to eat a lunch I could neither taste nor swallow, and then hugged him hard and drove away.

Without him.

While it was the first time for this child to go away to school, it was not the first time I've stumbled through this rite of passage. It doesn't get easier. In some ways it gets harder. Now I know how fraught with peril those college years are.

Still, I didn't float him down the Nile in a desperate attempt to save his life; I paid a formidable sum of money to entrust him to an institution that promises to educate him. His life is not in immediate danger. Or is it? College campuses aren't exactly without snares of the devil.

Jochabed's is the story for every woman who has ever worried about someone she loves, someone she wants to protect with all her power and might. But here's the thing: this is also the story for every woman who learns that she really doesn't have much power or might at all when it comes to the outcomes of the lives of her loved ones.

I don't think that I am the only mother who has been so overcome by worry for her child that I could not bear the thought of letting him go. I don't think that I'm the only one who has learned that life for our children can be difficult, and that we cannot protect them from hard knocks. I'm not the only one who has learned through years of parenting that sometimes things are even worse than we imagined they could be.

With all those lessons has come also the knowledge that fear is the enemy of growth—for the child and for me. Fear can thwart God's plan. And oh, does he ever have a plan! I've learned to recognize the level of control I have (often very little) and to stop struggling for more. I've learned to recognize if it's a real fear or if I've given my imagination far too much leeway. I've tried with varying degrees of success to starve the fear instead of letting it "free-range" in my imagination. Most of all, I've learned to recognize that we are each God's own son or daughter. He will give good gifts to his children—all his children. Above all, he will give the Holy Spirit, if only we ask. And so, I've learned to ask again and again and again that God be the parent I cannot be.

I cannot imagine the excruciating pain that came with both fear and sorrow coursing through Jochabed's veins during the first three months of Moses' life. I can't imagine the evenings she rocked her baby and contemplated his inevitable death at the hands of a pharaoh's army who had been commanded to drown all newborn boys. Did she move back and forth with the rhythm of her nursing babe and try to come up with a scheme that would let him live? When the time came, the best she could do was put him in a basket and float him in the river—and hope and pray.

Jochabed had no idea how God was to move in the life of her sweet infant. She didn't know that he would grow into the prophet God used to free the Hebrew people from slavery. She didn't even know that God would step in shortly after that basket touched the water with a plan that saved her son's life, provided for his future, and even allowed her to continue to nurse him. All she knew when she relinquished the baby in the basket to the mighty Nile was the movement of tender surrender.

For every mother who has ever acknowledged the limits of her control, Jochabed bears witness to this prayer: Dear Lord, thank you for the gift of this child. I know you love him more than I ever could. And I also know that you know how very much I love him—with every beat of my heart, so deeply that I feel like that heart will burst. And it is precisely because I love him so much that I surrender him to your plan, to your care, to your omnipresent protection. Please pour your grace upon him and keep him for yourself.

Elizabeth Foss

GIFTED & GRACED

ON THE DIGNITY AND VOCATION OF WOMEN

The moral and spiritual strength of a woman is joined to her awareness that God entrusts the human being to her in a special way. Of course, God entrusts every human being to each and every other human being. But this entrusting concerns women in a special way—precisely by reason of their femininity—and this in a particular way determines their vocation. (30)

CONTEMPLATIO

What conversion of mind, heart, and life is the Lord asking of me?

ACTIO

Is there someone in your life that God might have entrusted to you in this moment specifically so you would be the one to carry him or her back to God and let the Holy Spirit do his work in that heart? What do you need to let go of in order to fully surrender this person to God?

Day Seventeen
DAILY SCRIPTURE

Then one of the leaders of the synagogue named Jairus came and, when he saw him, fell at his feet and begged him repeatedly, "My little daughter is at the point of death. Come and lay your hands on her, so that she may be made well, and live." So he went with him.

And a large crowd followed him and pressed in on him. Now there was a woman who had been suffering from hemorrhages for twelve years. She had endured much under many physicians, and had spent all that she had; and she was no better, but rather grew worse. She had heard about Jesus, and came up behind him in the crowd and touched his cloak, for she said, "If I but touch his clothes, I will be made well." Immediately her hemorrhage stopped; and she felt in her body that she was healed of her disease. Immediately aware that power had gone forth from him, Jesus turned about in the crowd and said, "Who touched my clothes?" And his disciples said to him, "You see the crowd pressing in on you; how can you say, 'Who touched me?'" He looked all around to see who had done it. But the woman, knowing what had happened to her, came in fear and trembling, fell down before him, and told him the whole truth. He said to her, "Daughter, your faith has made you well; go in peace, and be healed of your disease."

While he was still speaking, some people came from the leader's house to say, "Your daughter is dead. Why trouble the teacher any further?" But overhearing what they said, Jesus said to the leader of the synagogue, "Do not fear, only believe." He allowed no one to follow him except Peter, James, and John, the brother of James. When they came to the house of the leader of the synagogue, he saw a commotion, people weeping and wailing loudly. When he had entered, he said to them, "Why do you make a commotion and weep? The child is not dead but sleeping." And they laughed at him. Then he put them all outside, and took the child's father and mother and those who were with him, and went in where the child was. He took her by the hand and said to her, "Talitha cum," which means, "Little girl, get up!" And immediately the girl got up and began to walk about (she was twelve years of age). At this they were overcome with amazement. He strictly ordered them that no one should know this, and told them to give her something to eat.

MARK 5:22-43

FOR FURTHER STUDY

Acts 9:39-41

CALL ME BLESSED

Jairus was a ruler in the synagogue of Capernaum—a man with religious authority and public respect. Yet in this moment, as his twelve-year-old daughter lay dying, he was simply a desperate father. Jesus' reputation as a miracle worker erased any fear Jairus may have had of him as a challenge to the religious authorities of the day. Jairus' great need, as well as his great faith, give us a unique glimpse of the heart of Jesus in one of the most memorable stories of the New Testament.

JAIRUS' DAUGHTER

LECTIO

In one word, she is . . .

What is her role in Scripture?

☐ Wife ☐ Listener
☐ Mother ☐ Sinner
☐ Daughter ☐ Friend
☐ Teacher ☐ Other:__________

What does God ask of her?

MEDITATIO

What does she teach me about the nature of God?

What does she teach me about being a woman of God?

ORATIO

How does her story impact mine?

The story of Jairus' daughter and the hemorrhaging woman is so captivating; it almost plays out like a film. Two women sought Jesus, and in his mercy, he healed them both, different though they were. On the surface, the stories may seem to overlap only coincidentally, but the Lord doesn't work that way. I wonder if there's a lesson we can learn in St. Mark's weaving together of these tales.

Imagine you're Jairus' daughter. You've never wanted for anything, and your father, an esteemed official, dotes on you, especially considering you live in a society where women are often treated poorly. Now, though, you've become sick and are wasting away, and there's nothing he can do but seek help from a stranger. Clinging to a shred of hope, your father leaves your side to seek out the Nazarene everyone is talking about—the one who performs signs—and to beg him to help you.

Now, imagine you're the bleeding woman. According to Mosaic law, your hemorrhage has made you ritually unclean for a dozen years (see Leviticus 15:19). You've been an outcast, unable even to seek the solace of the synagogue. You've unsuccessfully sought help from physicians, and you've found yourself searching for a miracle. Now you're so close. Amidst the throng clamoring for Jesus, you're buffeted and jostled. Desperately, you reach out to touch the hem of his robe.

Their stories don't seem so dissimilar after all, do they? They were both broken and in need of his healing. Let's explore the different parts of their stories.

According to *John Hardon's Catholic Dictionary: An Abridged and Updated Edition of Modern Catholic Dictionary*, the number twelve in the Bible signifies totality or maturity. For example, there are twelve tribes of Israel and the twelve apostles of Jesus. Did you notice that the bleeding woman hemorrhaged for twelve years and that Jairus' daughter was twelve years old? I wonder if St. Mark wanted us to know that these women had both reached their limits. The hemorrhaging woman suffered through twelve years of physical and emotional pain, and Jairus's daughter's life ended, perhaps abruptly, at age twelve.

Along came Jesus, the Divine Physician, just when these women had reached their limits, had suffered the totality of their illnesses. He disrupted the course of their lives, and he did so in order to heal and save them.

But how did Jesus go about healing them?

When the bleeding woman touched Jesus' cloak, he felt the power go out of him. She was healed by her faith and by Jesus' words: "Daughter, your faith has made you well; go in peace, and be healed of your disease" (Mark 5:34). This is a beautiful echo of the Father's plan for salvation. The Israelites reached out for God's power (see Judges 10:15), and God responded by speaking the Word, his Son, into the world to heal and deliver us all.

Finally arriving at Jairus' home, it appeared Jesus was too late. The little girl was already dead. Jesus, undaunted, performed an unfathomable miracle: he brought her back from the dead. What was his method? Again, he healed with his words by responding to Jairus' faith.

For some special reason, St. Mark preserved the Aramaic here. I always get weepy when I read those words, "Talitha cum." Jesus, in his native language, said, "Little girl, get up!" (Mark 5:41). Perhaps St. Mark wanted to give a precious gift to women down through the ages. How sweet it is to hear those words, to close our eyes and imagine that we are Jesus' little girl. With his tender voice, he calls us. "Little girl, get up," and just like that, we are fully alive again.

We see, then, through the intertwining of these stories, how we are all hemorrhaging women, how we are all beloved daughters. We see that the only way toward eternal life is through the healing words of Jesus Christ.

Micaela Darr

GIFTED & GRACED

ON THE DIGNITY AND VOCATION OF WOMEN

Unless we refer to this order and primacy we cannot give a complete and adequate answer to the question about women's dignity and vocation. When we say that the woman is the one who receives love in order to love in return, this refers not only or above all to the specific spousal relationship of marriage. It means something more universal, based on the very fact of her being a woman within all the interpersonal relationships which, in the most varied ways, shape society and structure the interaction between all persons—men and women. In this broad and diversified context, a woman represents a particular value by the fact that she is a human person, and, at the same time, this particular person, by the fact of her femininity. This concerns each and every woman, independently of the cultural context in which she lives, and independently of her spiritual, psychological and physical characteristics, as for example, age, education, health, work, and whether she is married or single. (29)

CONTEMPLATIO

What conversion of mind, heart, and life is the Lord asking of me?

ACTIO

To receive is not a passive act. The woman who opens herself to love and then pours that love out onto others is actively responding. She is alert and ready to receive what Christ offers in order to be fully alive. What is God offering to you today? How will you respond?

Day Eighteen

DAILY SCRIPTURE

I commend to you our sister Phoebe, a deacon of the church at Cenchreae, so that you may welcome her in the Lord as is fitting for the saints, and help her in whatever she may require from you, for she has been a benefactor of many and of myself as well.

ROMANS 16:1-2

FOR FURTHER STUDY

Galatians 3:23-24, 27-29

CALL ME BLESSED

As he ends his letter to the Romans, Paul sends greetings to many people. The section begins with the commendation of a woman named **Phoebe**, whom Paul calls "a deacon of the church" in her community (16:1). The term "deacon" is used in the New Testament for ordained ministers as well as more broadly for other servants and those in ministry. While we cannot be sure exactly what role this servant-leader played, Phoebe's service to the church is clearly significant in Paul's eyes as he exhorts the community in Rome to extend her generous hospitality.

PHOEBE

LECTIO

In one word, she is . . .

What is her role in Scripture?

- ☐ Wife
- ☐ Mother
- ☐ Daughter
- ☐ Teacher
- ☐ Listener
- ☐ Sinner
- ☐ Friend
- ☐ Other:__________

What does God ask of her?

MEDITATIO

What does she teach me about the nature of God?

What does she teach me about being a woman of God?

ORATIO

How does her story impact mine?

When people encountered Jesus in the Gospels, anyone who came with an open heart left changed. After looking into his eyes, their lives were entirely different. Still, there is no formula, no series of steps necessary to achieve a one-size-fits-all holiness. Some who met Jesus were called to follow, others sent home. Some were told to announce all that the Lord had done for them, others ordered to keep silent. Some were told to sell all that they had, and others heard no such command.

Those who met Jesus in the decades after his ascension were similarly diverse. While a few were called to go out to the ends of the earth, most were charged with ordinary holiness. Instead of preaching to the nations and earning a martyr's crown, they were asked to live in imitation of the hidden life at Nazareth, called to a radically new way of being what they already were.

Most of the women mentioned in Acts and the Pauline Epistles fit well into the established roles offered to them. They served the Church as mothers and grandmothers and offered hospitality by hosting the Church of God in their homes. And while they were honored and respected in a profoundly new way because of the Christian insistence that in Christ there is a fundamental equality between women and men, most served through those traditionally feminine roles.

And then there's Phoebe.

Phoebe was a *diakonos*, a servant of the Church who worked in ministry to other believers. While it's the same word as the ordained office of deacon, Paul uses the word almost exclusively in the broader sense of minister or servant. In calling Phoebe *diakonos*, he's describing her role, not as a purveyor of sacraments, but as a leader in the Church, one who spoke with the wisdom of the Spirit and drew souls to Christ.

Phoebe was a disciple whose holiness made her worthy to be called "sister" by Paul, a coworker in the vineyard of the Lord. Even the word here translated "benefactor" (Romans 16:2) rings with a sense of authority; more than just a woman who hosts charity auctions, Phoebe was a protector or guardian of those she served. Paul himself acknowledged her influence (and perhaps even direction) in his life.

Even those of us who are used to the idea of women serving in ministry may be taken aback when we consider the deference Paul showed to Phoebe; imagine, then, how his contemporaries felt. Though women were respected within their own domains, this type of public role, in which she exercised leadership even over such a one as Paul, was unheard of. She must have experienced tremendous opposition, from those within the fledgling Christian community as well as from unbelievers.

For Paul, as for Jesus, there was no issue. Phoebe was a child of God, and though she could not be called to the priesthood, there was a particular gift she could exercise in ministry precisely as a woman. She stands at the head of the litany of strong female saints in whose footsteps we follow: empresses, abbesses, doctors of the Church, preachers, and theologians, all women who did the will of God despite the world's opposition.

While Eunice, Nympha, and Lydia remind us of the beauty of an ordinary life offered to the Lord, Phoebe beckons in a different way. She invites us all to reflect on our own calling, to ask the Lord if there isn't something more he wants of us, some new way of serving that might make us—or others—uncomfortable. She reminds us that while many of us are called to live in holy obscurity, all of us are invited to serve as ministers to those entrusted to us by the Father. There is no one-size-fits-all path to holiness, but there are thousands of holy women who have gone before, blazing a thousand different trails and showing us how to blaze our own.

Meg Hunter-Kilmer

GIFTED & GRACED

ON THE DIGNITY AND VOCATION OF WOMEN

The personal resources of femininity are certainly no less than the resources of masculinity: they are merely different. Hence a woman, as well as a man, must understand her "fulfilment" as a person, her dignity and vocation, on the basis of these resources, according to the richness of the femininity which she received on the day of creation and which she inherits as an expression of the "image and likeness of God" that is specifically hers. (10)

CONTEMPLATIO

What conversion of mind, heart, and life is the Lord asking of me?

ACTIO

What is your calling, and what are your resources? Ask the Lord if there is something more he wants of you, some new way of serving that might make you uncomfortable, that might require you to draw more completely on the resources he gives you. Remember that while many of us are called to live in holy obscurity, all of us are invited to serve as ministers to those entrusted to us by the Father. How will you minister today? Next week? Next year?

Day Nineteen

DAILY SCRIPTURE

The words of King Lemuel. An oracle that his mother taught him:

No, my son! No, son of my womb!
  No, son of my vows!
Do not give your strength to women,
  your ways to those who destroy kings.
It is not for kings, O Lemuel,
  it is not for kings to drink wine,
  or for rulers to desire strong drink;
or else they will drink and forget what has been decreed,
  and will pervert the rights of all the afflicted.
Give strong drink to one who is perishing,
  and wine to those in bitter distress;
let them drink and forget their poverty,
  and remember their misery no more.
Speak out for those who cannot speak,
  for the rights of all the destitute.
Speak out, judge righteously,
  defend the rights of the poor and needy.

A capable wife who can find?
  She is far more precious than jewels.
The heart of her husband trusts in her,
  and he will have no lack of gain.
She does him good, and not harm,
  all the days of her life.
She seeks wool and flax,
  and works with willing hands.
She is like the ships of the merchant,
  she brings her food from far away.
She rises while it is still night
  and provides food for her household
  and tasks for her servant-girls.
She considers a field and buys it;
  with the fruit of her hands she plants a vineyard.
She girds herself with strength,
  and makes her arms strong.
She perceives that her merchandise is profitable.
  Her lamp does not go out at night.
She puts her hands to the distaff,
  and her hands hold the spindle.
She opens her hand to the poor,
  and reaches out her hands to the needy.
She is not afraid for her household when it snows,
  for all her household are clothed in crimson.
She makes herself coverings;
  her clothing is fine linen and purple.
Her husband is known in the city gates,
  taking his seat among the elders of the land.
She makes linen garments and sells them;
  she supplies the merchant with sashes.
Strength and dignity are her clothing,
  and she laughs at the time to come.
She opens her mouth with wisdom,
  and the teaching of kindness is on her tongue.
She looks well to the ways of her household,
  and does not eat the bread of idleness.
Her children rise up and call her happy;
  her husband too, and he praises her:
"Many women have done excellently,
  but you surpass them all."
Charm is deceitful, and beauty is vain,
  but a woman who fears the LORD is to be praised.
Give her a share in the fruit of her hands,
  and let her works praise her in the city gates.

PROVERBS 31

FOR FURTHER STUDY

1 Peter 3:1-6; Ephesians 5:22–6:9

CALL ME BLESSED

The description of womanhood here in Proverbs 31 is noted as a prophecy of King Lemuel taught by his mother. While history does not denote exactly who King Lemuel was, we do know that in Jewish history, a king's mother held a place of high honor, and her counsel was highly respected. This woman would have borne the title Queen Mother. The teaching about the wide spectrum of gifts and grace women offer was meant to be disseminated widely as motherly wisdom for a kingdom, as well as now for all generations of Christian women who follow in the footsteps of that wisdom.

PROVERBS 31 WOMAN

LECTIO

In one word, she is . . .

What is her role in Scripture?

- ☐ Wife
- ☐ Mother
- ☐ Daughter
- ☐ Teacher
- ☐ Listener
- ☐ Sinner
- ☐ Friend
- ☐ Other:__________

What does God ask of her?

MEDITATIO

What does she teach me about the nature of God?

What does she teach me about being a woman of God?

ORATIO

How does her story impact mine?

The first time I heard the description of the woman in Proverbs 31, I was at a friend's wedding. I was newly engaged, dreaming of my own wedding and marriage with excited anticipation. But anxiety began to creep into my mind as what sounded like a checklist for the perfect woman and wife from Proverbs was read. Was anyone actually like this ideal woman? Who could possibly embody all of those incredible attributes? This perfect woman indeed seemed perfect. But she also seemed unrealistic. And frankly? Her perfection kind of annoyed me.

As I reflected on what kind of wife I wanted to be, supportive and loving came to mind, of course. And I hoped that my husband would always trust me as I trusted him—that we could guide each other through life and, hopefully, to heaven. But on top of that, could I also expertly care for my home and everyone in it so well as to have no worries? Could I become a savvy businesswoman, be strong enough to do good work with my hands, always speak kindly and care for the poor, and still be energetic enough to work late, rise early, and never "eat the bread of idleness," among other things (Proverbs 31:27)? It didn't seem likely, and I'd need a whole lot of God's grace to even start trying.

But in getting so caught up in all the incredible attributes of the Proverbs 31 woman, I missed what is mentioned after all that: her fear of the Lord. She is to be praised, not because of her impressive résumé and skill set, but because of what drives her to do all those things.

Her fear of the Lord doesn't pull her away from God, causing her to constantly worry about what he thinks of her or what he will do if she stumbles in sin. Rather, it's a fear born out of her love for God—a fear of not being close to the Lord she loves. This fear doesn't paralyze; rather, it spurs action, pushing her to seek God and to follow his path for her life as best she can. And as she draws close to him, she discovers a strength not of her own, which allows her to do and become what would otherwise be impossible.

Like the Proverbs 31 woman, we can use our fear of a life of sin and separation from God to drive us to continuously seek him, hope in him, and trust in his promises. And as we deepen our relationship with God, he will strengthen us too. Over time, we'll find ourselves doing things we know we could never do on our own, and we'll sense that we're growing ever closer to becoming the women he means for us to be. It's not about being perfect or living up to a specific set of attributes and accomplishments; it's about aligning our hearts with God, which in and of itself will bear remarkable fruit, unique to each one of us. As St. John Paul II said, "Woman transcends all expectations when her heart is faithful to God" (General Audience, April 10, 1996).

At the end of our lives, our list of attributes and accomplishments will surely be different from those of the Proverbs 31 woman. But when we strive to embrace a life of service and love to which God calls us, then we, too, can live in hope that our loved ones will one day rise and call us blessed. For when we reflect God's love for us to others, we become a source of support and strength for them. And it is then that we can live in hope of drawing, not only our family closer to God, but also those who are broken and lost in the world.

Allison McGinley

GIFTED & GRACED

ON THE DIGNITY AND VOCATION OF WOMEN

Thus the "perfect woman" (cf. Prov 31:10) becomes an irreplaceable support and source of spiritual strength for other people, who perceive the great energies of her spirit. These "perfect women" are owed much by their families, and sometimes by whole nations. (30)

CONTEMPLATIO

What conversion of mind, heart, and life is the Lord asking of me?

ACTIO

Put pen to paper, and make a list of the ways God strengthens you, the things you do that you know you could not possibly do on your own. Then, make a new list of things you hope to do with Jesus' help.

Day Twenty

DAILY SCRIPTURE

Then Laban said to Jacob, "Because you are my kinsman, should you therefore serve me for nothing? Tell me, what shall your wages be?" Now Laban had two daughters; the name of the elder was Leah, and the name of the younger was Rachel. Leah's eyes were lovely, and Rachel was graceful and beautiful. Jacob loved Rachel; so he said, "I will serve you seven years for your younger daughter Rachel." Laban said, "It is better that I give her to you than that I should give her to any other man; stay with me." So Jacob served seven years for Rachel, and they seemed to him but a few days because of the love he had for her.

Then Jacob said to Laban, "Give me my wife that I may go in to her, for my time is completed." So Laban gathered together all the people of the place, and made a feast. But in the evening he took his daughter Leah and brought her to Jacob; and he went in to her. (Laban gave his maid Zilpah to his daughter Leah to be her maid.) When morning came, it was Leah! And Jacob said to Laban, "What is this you have done to me? Did I not serve with you for Rachel? Why then have you deceived me?" Laban said, "This is not done in our country—giving the younger before the firstborn. Complete the week of this one, and we will give you the other also in return for serving me another seven years." Jacob did so, and completed her week; then Laban gave him his daughter Rachel as a wife. (Laban gave his maid Bilhah to his daughter Rachel to be her maid.) So Jacob went in to Rachel also, and he loved Rachel more than Leah. He served Laban for another seven years.

When the LORD saw that Leah was unloved, he opened her womb; but Rachel was barren. Leah conceived and bore a son, and she named him Reuben; for she said, "Because the LORD has looked on my affliction; surely now my husband will love me." She conceived again and bore a son, and said, "Because the LORD has heard that I am hated, he has given me this son also"; and she named him Simeon. Again she conceived and bore a son, and said, "Now this time my husband will be joined to me, because I have borne him three sons"; therefore he was named Levi. She conceived again and bore a son, and said, "This time I will praise the LORD"; therefore she named him Judah; then she ceased bearing.

GENESIS 29:15-35

FOR FURTHER STUDY

Luke 7:36-50; 1 Samuel 16:7

CALL ME BLESSED

Leah was the firstborn daughter of Laban, and her sister was Rachel. Jacob desired Rachel as his wife, but Laban tricked him into marrying Leah first. After a week, Rachel became his second wife. Leah was able to have children quickly and easily, and she bore Jacob six sons and a daughter before Rachel gave birth to Joseph and Benjamin. Leah's son Levi was the ancestor of the tribe of Levi, which was entrusted with worship and education in religious matters. Her son Judah was the patriarch of the tribe of Judah, making her an ancestor of all the Davidic kings and eventually of Jesus.

LEAH

LECTIO

In one word, she is . . .

What is her role in Scripture?

- ☐ Wife
- ☐ Mother
- ☐ Daughter
- ☐ Teacher
- ☐ Listener
- ☐ Sinner
- ☐ Friend
- ☐ Other:__________

What does God ask of her?

MEDITATIO

What does she teach me about the nature of God?

What does she teach me about being a woman of God?

ORATIO

How does her story impact mine?

The scene still burns in my memory. My mother is frantically wringing her hands and talking about how it's all so embarrassing. My father's eyes dart from her to me, alternating between annoyance (at her) and sympathy (for me). It was late spring of my senior year of high school, ten days before the prom I'd been elected by my peers to plan. I might mention that it was also the eighties, and people only went to prom with a date. I had a date. And then I didn't. My date was taking someone else.

I offered to my distraught mother that I might call my friend Tim, who'd graduated the previous year. My father's eyes lit up with the excitement of a man who was sure he could solve the problem.

My father, who'd always insisted I earn all my spending money, said, "Tell him I'll pay for dinner. And the ticket. And his tux. And gas money. Whatever it takes."

Whatever it takes. I'll do whatever it takes to be sure there's a young man by your side, because clearly, no one will take you unless I fix it so that they do.

Tim took me, and he was a really good sport about it. But I've never forgotten that my dad had to sort of cheat to get me a date to my senior prom.

If you have ever felt unwanted and unlovable, ever felt like you fall short of other people's ideals (and been bitterly disappointed when they fall short of yours), Leah is your girl.

Leah knew what it was like to miss out on the man. No one was lining up to want to marry her. Instead, Jacob begged Leah's father for the hand of her sister, Rachel. After Jacob worked seven years to win Rachel's hand, the girls' father, Laban, tricked him and tucked Leah under the bridal veil. When Jacob discovered he'd been duped, he didn't give up. He kept Leah but took Rachel as his second wife a week later, after agreeing to work for Laban another seven years in order to earn the girl he really wanted. And all that time, Leah knew that she wasn't second choice; she wasn't even a choice at all. Scripture tells us that she was not as beautiful as Rachel, and that she was unloved.

God saw Leah's pain, and he had compassion on her. He also had a plan for her. God opened Leah's womb, and she bore six sons and a daughter. The fourth of those sons was Judah, who would be pivotal in the happy resolution of the story of Joseph. Judah was the patriarch of the royal tribe in Israel that established David as king. And the Messiah came from the line of David.

Of course, Leah didn't know that one day she would be remembered as a woman "who . . . built up the house of Israel" (Ruth 4:11). She simply acknowledged that despite the continued rejection of her husband, the Lord was blessing her abundantly as he filled her womb with new life. So even in her sorrow, she praised her God. God met her there—in her tear-soaked praise—and lavished love on her.

We have a choice when faced with the sorrow that comes with the world's rejection. We can succumb to seeing ourselves as unwanted and unloved, or we can see ourselves as beloved daughters of a good Father. We can choose to believe that his plan is infinitely better than any we can imagine and that he has created us for a purpose that is entirely good and entirely beautiful.

It's his vision.
His plan.
His understanding of our beauty and our value.

Even the people we hold closest to us will fail on occasion, and we will doubt their love and yearn for their affirmation. God alone can be trusted to love in full, always. He asks us to trust him to write love into the most painful pages of our life.

Four years after my senior prom, I returned to the same venue as a chaperone for my little sister's prom. My date was the boy who canceled on me for my own prom, and we spent the evening with our former teachers, showing off my engagement ring (with the stone shaped like a perfect shining tear) and chatting about wedding plans. Turns out the God who can redeem everything enjoys irony and has a lovely sense of story.

Elizabeth Foss

GIFTED & GRACED

ON THE DIGNITY AND VOCATION OF WOMEN

Each woman therefore is "the only creature on earth which God willed for its own sake." Each of them from the "beginning" inherits as a woman the dignity of personhood. Jesus of Nazareth confirms this dignity, recalls it, renews it, and makes it a part of the Gospel and of the Redemption for which he is sent into the world. Every word and gesture of Christ about women must therefore be brought into the dimension of the Paschal Mystery. In this way everything is completely explained. (13)

CONTEMPLATIO

What conversion of mind, heart, and life is the Lord asking of me?

ACTIO

Your dignity is not dependent on anyone else's affirmation of you. It is not dependent on a ring on your finger or a corner office or an advanced degree. It is not dependent on the birth of your children or their successful launch into the world. You inherited your dignity. It lives and breathes in you. How will it manifest itself today?

SELAH

Use this day for pause, prayer, praise, and rest.

Weekly Check-In

THE BEST TIME TO STUDY	A PLACE I FIND QUIET
________________	________________

AS I STUDY *CALL ME BLESSED*, I'M FEELING

○ *happy*	○ *anxious*	○ *annoyed*	○ *grateful*	○ ________
○ *excited*	○ *upset*	○ *angry*	○ *confused*	○ ________
○ *joyful*	○ *tired*	○ *sad*	○ *calm*	○ ________

My heart is changing:

God is changing:

Scripture I can't shake:

A woman of God I want to reflect:

Women in my prayers:

Asking for Mary's intercession:

Grateful for:

Day Twenty-Two

MEMORY VERSE

ISAIAH 66:13

I will practice Scripture memory by

- ◯ Praying
- ◯ Writing
- ◯ Speaking
- ◯ Reading
- ◯ Other: ________________

AS A MOTHER
COMFORTS
HER CHILD,
SO I WILL
COMFORT YOU;
YOU SHALL BE
COMFORTED IN
JERUSALEM.

Day Twenty-Three

DAILY SCRIPTURE

Greet Prisca and Aquila, who work with me in Christ Jesus, and who risked their necks for my life, to whom not only I give thanks, but also all the churches of the Gentiles. Greet also the church in their house. Greet my beloved Epaenetus, who was the first convert in Asia for Christ.

ROMANS 16:3-5

The churches of Asia send greetings. Aquila and Prisca, together with the church in their house, greet you warmly in the Lord. All the brothers and sisters send greetings. Greet one another with a holy kiss.

1 CORINTHIANS 16:19-20

FOR FURTHER STUDY

Acts 18; 2 Timothy 4:16-22; Romans 16:3

CALL ME BLESSED

Prisca and Aquila, a prominent couple in the early Church, are greeted by Paul in his letter to the Romans and are accompanying him as he writes his first letter to the Corinthians in which they send their greeting to the new church. On both occasions, it is noted that there is a whole church community based out of their home. Clearly, these servants of God contributed much to the growth of the early Church and were trusted leaders in Paul's eyes. And Prisca is noted equally with her husband for that service.

PRISCA

LECTIO

In one word, she is . . .

What is her role in Scripture?

☐ Wife ☐ Listener
☐ Mother ☐ Sinner
☐ Daughter ☐ Friend
☐ Teacher ☐ Other:__________

What does God ask of her?

MEDITATIO

What does she teach me about the nature of God?

What does she teach me about being a woman of God?

ORATIO

How does her story impact mine?

These are days of growth and change in our Church. There is a groundswell, a gathering of voices seeking to bring about something beautiful from the cloud of darkness and despair. What can the modern woman learn from a woman of the early Church about how to contribute meaningfully to its growth and well-being?

With authority and urgency, Prisca's story calls women into the importance of the moment. Prisca and her husband, Aquila, bear witness to a vocation that encourages us and challenges us. Though they did not meet Jesus before his death, they heard and answered him and let him shape their lives in radical ways. In doing so, they helped to shape the early Church.

They opened their home to Paul, offering him both shelter and work. The couple believed the Lord when he promised to protect Paul, and then they offered themselves as instruments in keeping that promise. When Paul left Corinth for Syria, they went with him, again opening their home to God's plans, establishing a church in their house so that early Christians could meet to pray and worship. And when the well-educated Apollos arrived, teaching an incomplete message about Jesus, Prisca and Aquila together instructed him in the fullness of the faith, shaping the future of Apollos' teaching ministry to conform more perfectly to the gospel message.

Prisca was a woman who knew her gifts and used them to their utmost potential, thereby impacting "all the churches of the Gentiles" (Romans 16:4). What extraordinary reach! She recognized that her feminine attributes were a gift to the early church, but she also provided a vivid model for working alongside men to broaden and deepen the kingdom. She was not limited by preconceived notions of her role or even of how her life should look. Instead, she lived from one inspiration of the Holy Spirit to the next, responding with one brave step after another.

Her story teaches us that our feminine gifts are uniquely bestowed by God, imbued in our souls so that we can unbox them, explore them, cultivate them, and elevate them. Each of us is gifted differently, each of us called to use those gifts in particular ways to further the kingdom. Prisca was a woman who lived a life of fruitful prayer that helped her to understand well what her unique gifts were. Then she was obedient and brave and disciplined enough to use them to their fullest potential. Like other women of her time, she created and kept a home, and she clearly invited others into that home hospitably. From that place of refuge (in Rome particularly, it was literally a safe haven from mortal peril), she reached out, and she shared the gospel.

The Church was young, and its structure was mostly undefined. Prisca had no female Christian role models. She looked to the Holy Spirit and let him call her. When he asked her to teach a learned man in order to show him how limited his knowledge of Christ was, she did. And that was extraordinary in her day! She wasn't limited by preconceived notions of roles. Because of her boldness and the clarity of God's unique message to her, all the churches were blessed by her teaching, her leadership, her sacrifice. Was she surprised by the way God used her to further the kingdom?

How will he use you? As you sit there today, pondering Prisca's story and considering the Church of our day—how will God ask you to stretch beyond yourself and open your doors? How will you further the Church in your home? How will you travel for him? As God speaks to you, don't interrupt him with your planner lists and your logistics. Instead, listen intently to the Spirit, and then ask him how to work out the logistical challenges for his glory. He'll show up. Hear him out before you tell him it's impossible.

Nothing is impossible with God.

Elizabeth Foss

GIFTED & GRACED

MORE WISDOM FROM ST. JOHN PAUL II

In his July 23, 1995 Angelus address, John Paul II said, "It is a 'sign of the times' that woman's role is increasingly recognized, not only in the family circle, but also in the wider context of all social activities. Without the contribution of women, society is less alive, culture impoverished, and peace less stable. Situations where women are prevented from developing their full potential and from offering the wealth of their gifts should therefore be considered profoundly unjust, not only to women themselves but to society as a whole."

CONTEMPLATIO

What conversion of mind, heart, and life is the Lord asking of me?

ACTIO

You are a force for peace. Further, you bring society to life, and you enrich the culture. Maybe your sphere of influence in these matters is small, and maybe it is wide. Whatever it is, it is yours. How will you develop your full potential there?

Day Twenty-Four

DAILY SCRIPTURE

Now as they went on their way, he entered a certain village, where a woman named Martha welcomed him into her home. She had a sister named Mary, who sat at the Lord's feet and listened to what he was saying. But Martha was distracted by her many tasks; so she came to him and asked, "Lord, do you not care that my sister has left me to do all the work by myself? Tell her then to help me." But the Lord answered her, "Martha, Martha, you are worried and distracted by many things; there is need of only one thing. Mary has chosen the better part, which will not be taken away from her."

LUKE 10:38-42

FOR FURTHER STUDY

Titus 2:1-15; Galatians 4:21-31

CALL ME BLESSED

Martha, the sister of Lazarus and Mary, is, along with her siblings, considered one of Jesus' dearest friends. While we often limit our impression of Martha to the busy woman seemingly rebuked by Jesus, Martha was clearly a prominent figure in the community of Bethany, whose home was always filled. Her great faith in Jesus and vulnerable connection with him were a witness to the people who looked to Martha's guidance that this man was truly more than the simple rabbi they saw with earthly eyes, that he was, indeed, the Messiah.

MARTHA

LECTIO

In one word, she is . . .

What is her role in Scripture?

- ☐ Wife
- ☐ Mother
- ☐ Daughter
- ☐ Teacher
- ☐ Listener
- ☐ Sinner
- ☐ Friend
- ☐ Other:__________

What does God ask of her?

MEDITATIO

What does she teach me about the nature of God?

What does she teach me about being a woman of God?

ORATIO

How does her story impact mine?

"Martha, Martha, you are worried and distracted by many things" (Luke 10:41).

How many times have I scurried about my house, picking up toys here, washing a dish there, and recited those words to myself? Sometimes I graciously take it as an admonishment from the Lord. Be mindful. Be slow and deliberate. Other moments, I roll my eyes in jest at my Lord.

"You gave me all these children, Lord. You'd better believe I'm distracted by them!"

Who was Martha of Bethany, though, and what can we learn from her? In John 11:5, we read, "Jesus loved Martha and her sister and Lazarus," so we know Jesus had affection for her, as well as for her siblings.

We also know Martha had a great faith in Jesus. In John 11:21-22, we read that "Martha said to Jesus, 'Lord, if you had been here, my brother would not have died. But even now I know that God will give you whatever you ask of him.'"

Think about that for a minute. Her brother had been dead and buried for four days. As an ancient Israelite, Martha would have been close enough to death to understand the level of decomposition his body would have already undergone. And still, she knew that if Jesus but asked his heavenly Father to raise Lazarus from the dead, the desire would be granted. That, my friends, is faith and hope in the Lord.

Knowing that Martha was beloved of Jesus and a woman of great faith, in what light do we see her complaint about Mary, and Jesus' gentle admonishment in return? Historically, biblical scholars have considered Luke 10:38-42 as an allegory for the spiritual life (see *CCC*, 2709–2731). Mary is the life of contemplative prayer, while Martha is prayer lived out through acts of service.

Rumer Godden's book *In This House of Brede* has a brief debate among the Benedictine nuns about whether it is better to be a missionary sister or a cloistered nun:

> *"The Church needs many, many Marthas," Dame Clare said gently, laying her hand on Julian's.*
> *"Yes!" cried Julian. "Look at the state of the world."*
> *"Which is why she needs a few Marys too."*

Few women are called to a purely contemplative life, but none of us are called to a life solely of service, devoid of relationship with God. For the majority of women, a healthy spirituality lies in finding the balance between Martha and Mary. What I believe Jesus is trying to teach Martha in that moment is that for our works to bear fruit, we must first sit at Jesus' feet, learn his teachings. Only then will we be equipped to step out into the world with hands ready to serve him.

The encouraging part about Martha's story is that she was loved by Jesus, faithful to him, and had a heart for service, and yet still the Lord admonished her. I'm quite certain he did so out of love, not anger or frustration, and I appreciate it. So often when we read about the lives of saints, they seem practically perfect from birth. That definitely doesn't ring true for my life, so I'm happy to be able to identify with Martha.

Knowing that children need chastisement to grow in virtue, it's comforting to see Jesus rebuke Martha. As I often remind my own kids, if I didn't care about them, I wouldn't bother correcting them. I believe the same thing could be said about this exchange between Jesus and Martha.

If Mary is the heart, then Martha is the hands. Begin with Mary's heart of prayer, and then step out into the world with the determination, the fortitude, and the faith of Martha.

Can I accept Jesus' loving challenge to slow down and hear him? Can I put him first in all things and, only then, stand up and take his desires out into the world? St. Martha of Bethany, pray for us!

Micaela Darr

GIFTED & GRACED

ON THE DIGNITY AND VOCATION OF WOMEN

The moral and spiritual strength of a woman is joined to her awareness that God entrusts the human being to her in a special way. Of course, God entrusts every human being to each and every other human being. But this entrusting concerns women in a special way—precisely by reason of their femininity—and this in a particular way determines their vocation.

The moral force of women, which draws strength from this awareness and this entrusting, expresses itself in a great number of figures of the Old Testament, of the time of Christ, and of later ages right up to our own day.

A woman is strong because of her awareness of this entrusting, strong because of the fact that God "entrusts the human being to her," always and in every way, even in the situations of social discrimination in which she may find herself. This awareness and this fundamental vocation speak to women of the dignity which they receive from God himself, and this makes them "strong" and strengthens their vocation. (30)

CONTEMPLATIO

What conversion of mind, heart, and life is the Lord asking of me?

ACTIO

You have been entrusted with the care of other human beings, entrusted to bind their wounds and wipe their tears. Slow down and listen. With whom and how will you answer this sacred trust?

Day Twenty-Five

DAILY SCRIPTURE

The LORD dealt with Sarah as he had said, and the LORD did for Sarah as he had promised. Sarah conceived and bore Abraham a son in his old age, at the time of which God had spoken to him. Abraham gave the name Isaac to his son whom Sarah bore him. And Abraham circumcised his son Isaac when he was eight days old, as God had commanded him. Abraham was a hundred years old when his son Isaac was born to him. Now Sarah said, "God has brought laughter for me; everyone who hears will laugh with me." And she said, "Who would ever have said to Abraham that Sarah would nurse children? Yet I have borne him a son in his old age."

The child grew, and was weaned; and Abraham made a great feast on the day that Isaac was weaned.

GENESIS 21:1-8

Tell me, you who desire to be subject to the law, will you not listen to the law? For it is written that Abraham had two sons, one by a slave woman and the other by a free woman. One, the child of the slave, was born according to the flesh; the other, the child of the free woman, was born through the promise. Now this is an allegory: these women are two covenants. One woman, in fact, is Hagar, from Mount Sinai, bearing children for slavery. Now Hagar is Mount Sinai in Arabia and corresponds to the present Jerusalem, for she is in slavery with her children. But the other woman corresponds to the Jerusalem above; she is free, and she is our mother. For it is written,

> "Rejoice, you childless one, you who bear no children, burst into song and shout, you who endure no birth pangs; for the children of the desolate woman are more numerous than the children of the one who is married."

Now you, my friends, are children of the promise, like Isaac. But just as at that time the child who was born according to the flesh persecuted the child who was born according to the Spirit, so it is now also. But what does the scripture say? "Drive out the slave and her child; for the child of the slave will not share the inheritance with the child of the free woman." So then, friends, we are children, not of the slave but of the free woman.

GALATIANS 4:21-31

FOR FURTHER STUDY

Genesis 12:1-9; 16:1-6; 17:15-19; 18:9-15

CALL ME BLESSED

Sarah appears on the timeline of salvation history as part of God's covenant to renew his relationship with man and make a chosen nation of Israel. Abraham is to become the father of that nation, and Sarah, thus, the mother. Sarah's story is one fraught with imperfection and difficulty. Yet she stands throughout history as a great figure at the first point on the timeline that leads to our salvation in Christ, the woman through whom God brought forth the nation he would call his own when he walked the earth.

SARAH

LECTIO

In one word, she is . . .

What is her role in Scripture?

☐ Wife ☐ Listener
☐ Mother ☐ Sinner
☐ Daughter ☐ Friend
☐ Teacher ☐ Other:__________

What does God ask of her?

MEDITATIO

What does she teach me about the nature of God?

What does she teach me about being a woman of God?

ORATIO

How does her story impact mine?

As I squirted shampoo on his head, he screamed at me, face contorted in fury. Beads of water dripped off his nose, as if mocking his anger, and it took everything in me not to wipe them away. Fortunately, I knew that was the worst thing I could do in the moment. But that was really all I knew. The way I'd confidently approached helping this man with his everyday tasks, as if I knew best, had obviously been all wrong.

I was an idealistic twenty-two-year-old who'd longed to be a mother since I was a little girl. And I wanted to give the motherly love I felt inside to everyone, especially those who were marginalized and hurting. But I was naïve enough to think that I could just walk in, offer my love, and have it eagerly accepted. I had to learn the hard way that to give true, respectful love, I had to first let go of my agenda, expectations, and pretense. My ego had to be broken down. It was going to hurt, but it would be worth it.

This wisdom came while sharing a house with upwards of ten people, some with diagnosed developmental disabilities, all of us with real human weakness. Eventually, there came incredible joy and a sense of belonging like I'd never known. But first I had to embrace my own shortcomings and brokenness and humbly be rebuilt through God's love, reflected by those I shared life with.

Several years later, I was pregnant, ecstatic at finally getting the chance to mother a child of my own. But I miscarried after only a few weeks. Despite the shortness of my pregnancy, I knew I would never be the same. Although I never held my son, I knew I would forever be connected to him; I would always be his mother. And having shared in the incredible mystery of creating new life, I knew that my relationship with God was forever changed too. There was a new sense of partnership. My compassion for everyone around me deepened as I found myself increasingly able to see them as they're seen through God's eyes and through the eyes of a loving mother: precious and irreplaceable.

Sarah also longed to mother a child, to nurture and love in that intimate way, and she had to wait more than ninety years for her dream to come true. But she gave great love to others during that long wait, particularly to her husband, Abraham. She faithfully followed him as they left everything and became nomads, enduring famine and familial disputes, all while suffering the heartbreak of perpetually empty arms. She willingly let herself be broken again and again for love's sake. Then she was surprised by joy as a fulfilled promise grew in her womb and as she experienced that intimate, wondrous connection between herself and her child, and herself and God.

A woman who was barren for over ninety years may seem an unlikely candidate for the matriarch of the faith, but she really isn't at all. In God's perfect plan, he chose a woman whose innate feminine genius was so strong that it spurred her to love deeply as a spiritual mother before doing so as a physical mother.

As women, we are called to tap into our feminine genius and share nurturing, healing love with others. We might do this as spiritual mothers, physical mothers, or both. But it will always necessitate a willingness to be broken. Let us look to Sarah when we fear that pain, trusting that it is not meaningless. As her life shows us, God invites every woman to be an active part of his plan for the world. He has created us as uniquely capable of answering this call by enabling us to give love that is innately maternal, and that ultimately has the power to transform the world.

Allison McGinley

GIFTED & GRACED

ON THE DIGNITY AND VOCATION OF WOMEN

Motherhood involves a special communion with the mystery of life, as it develops in the woman's womb. The mother is filled with wonder at this mystery of life, and "understands" with unique intuition what is happening inside her. In the light of the "beginning," the mother accepts and loves as a person the child she is carrying in her womb. This unique contact with the new human being developing within her gives rise to an attitude towards human beings— not only towards her own child, but every human being—which profoundly marks the woman's personality. (18)

CONTEMPLATIO

What conversion of mind, heart, and life is the Lord asking of me?

ACTIO

We are all called to mother; we are all equipped with the ability to nurture and to love from a place of total self-giving. How will you love that way today?

Day Twenty-Six

DAILY SCRIPTURE

We set sail from Troas and took a straight course to Samothrace, the following day to Neapolis, and from there to Philippi, which is a leading city of the district of Macedonia and a Roman colony. We remained in this city for some days. On the sabbath day we went outside the gate by the river, where we supposed there was a place of prayer; and we sat down and spoke to the women who had gathered there. A certain woman named Lydia, a worshiper of God, was listening to us; she was from the city of Thyatira and a dealer in purple cloth. The Lord opened her heart to listen eagerly to what was said by Paul. When she and her household were baptized, she urged us, saying, "If you have judged me to be faithful to the Lord, come and stay at my home." And she prevailed upon us.

ACTS 16:11-15

FOR FURTHER STUDY

Philippians 1:3-11

CALL ME BLESSED

Lydia heard the good news from St. Paul at the river's edge in the territory of Macedonia. The waters of that river were the resource that made vibrant dyed fabric the area's main commerce. Lydia is noted as a skilled businesswoman in the sale of this fabric. She is also "a believer" in some sense, although she has not yet heard of Christ. Lydia's enthusiastic reception of the gospel and desire to bring baptism to her whole family gives her the distinction of being the first named European convert of St. Paul.

LYDIA

LECTIO

In one word, she is . . .

What is her role in Scripture?

☐ Wife ☐ Listener
☐ Mother ☐ Sinner
☐ Daughter ☐ Friend
☐ Teacher ☐ Other:__________

What does God ask of her?

MEDITATIO

What does she teach me about the nature of God?

What does she teach me about being a woman of God?

ORATIO

How does her story impact mine?

A lot can happen in the course of a normal day in our busy lives. Getting everyone fed, out of the house to where they need to be, heading to work—whether at home or beyond—and returning again to finish the day's tasks can leave me exhausted. Yet it is those ordinary things in my day that God uses to speak and move through me. It is in the regular business of the day that we meet and share Jesus.

In a day when modern culture has created a caricature of what it is to be a strong woman, I find great solace in the wisdom of the Church. I don't have to "do it all" according to someone else's checklist of what it means to be a successful woman. Embracing our true feminine genius is not to subject ourselves to some cookie-cutter model of the "perfect woman" or even a faithful one. It is to embrace all God has given us—our skills, our talents, our dreams, our situation in life—and use it for his glory. It is to be open to others. It is to create community. It is to encourage and uplift. It is to use our supernatural charisms for the good of our families, neighbors, communities, and world. We have a great power in our femininity, however that looks in our lives.

Take Lydia. Lydia is not only the first named European convert of St. Paul but is also believed by scholars to have helped St. Paul establish the first European house church through her invitation for them to "come and stay" (Acts 16:15). Lydia's pivotal role in the introduction of the gospel to Europe was born within what seemed to be an otherwise normal day.

We are told "the Lord opened her heart" (Acts 16:14) to listen eagerly to what St. Paul was preaching. There is no assumption that Lydia set out that day with a mission to bring the apostle home with her. She was simply at work, a skilled businesswoman and craftswoman of her day, dyeing expensive cloth to be sold to royalty. She worked in community with other women, possibly leading them in prayer and work. It is here that the Lord moves her heart through St. Paul's preaching.

Openness, communal leadership, responsive listening, and radical hospitality—these are the gifts Lydia offers. God works with these simple gifts to begin the spread of Christianity in Europe. It is our simple yes that continues the work of the gospel today. We have a great capacity as women to listen, encourage, and invite.

If we take a look at the state of the world today, we cannot doubt it is in desperate need of the good news. We need Jesus, and as women we have an inherent power to bring the gospel message of redemption, mercy, and hope to the world. Whether through serving our families at home, encouraging our colleagues at work, or speaking out against injustice in our neighborhoods and communities, we continue to plant the seeds of faith.

My husband always remarks that I have a greater openness to and trust in God's providence than he does. I usually just shrug that off. Yet it is that gift that allows our family to take risks, respond to God's call, and remain hopeful when things look bleak. Never underestimate the gifts you have been given, friends. While they may seem insignificant to you, they may be the very breath of life for someone else.

There are no small things in God's eyes. You don't have to conform yourself to a preconceived template of what it means to be a woman. God has given you exactly what he wishes to use. Every gift you have and share, he will multiply. Every skill you have been given, used in service for another, God will direct toward his glory. We have only to look, listen, and act in faith.

Rakhi McCormick

GIFTED & GRACED

ON THE DIGNITY AND VOCATION OF WOMEN

The hour is coming, in fact has come, when the vocation of women is being acknowledged in its fullness, the hour in which women acquire in the world an influence, an effect and a power never hitherto achieved. That is why, at this moment when the human race is undergoing so deep a transformation, women imbued with a spirit of the Gospel can do so much to aid humanity in not falling. (1)

CONTEMPLATIO

What conversion of mind, heart, and life is the Lord asking of me?

ACTIO

Open your heart to the Lord. In what ways will you listen, encourage, and invite?

Day Twenty-Seven
DAILY SCRIPTURE

David said to Abigail, "Blessed be the LORD, the God of Israel, who sent you to meet me today! Blessed be your good sense, and blessed be you, who have kept me today from bloodguilt and from avenging myself by my own hand! For as surely as the LORD the God of Israel lives, who has restrained me from hurting you, unless you had hurried and come to meet me, truly by morning there would not have been left to Nabal so much as one male." Then David received from her hand what she had brought him; he said to her, "Go up to your house in peace; see, I have heeded your voice, and I have granted your petition."

Abigail came to Nabal; he was holding a feast in his house, like the feast of a king. Nabal's heart was merry within him, for he was very drunk; so she told him nothing at all until the morning light. In the morning, when the wine had gone out of Nabal, his wife told him these things, and his heart died within him; he became like a stone. About ten days later the LORD struck Nabal, and he died.

When David heard that Nabal was dead, he said, "Blessed be the LORD who has judged the case of Nabal's insult to me, and has kept back his servant from evil; the LORD has returned the evildoing of Nabal upon his own head." Then David sent and wooed Abigail, to make her his wife. When David's servants came to Abigail at Carmel, they said to her, "David has sent us to you to take you to him as his wife." She rose and bowed down, with her face to the ground, and said, "Your servant is a slave to wash the feet of the servants of my lord." Abigail got up hurriedly and rode away on a donkey; her five maids attended her. She went after the messengers of David and became his wife.

1 SAMUEL 25:32-42

FOR FURTHER STUDY

1 Samuel 25:1-31

CALL ME BLESSED

Abigail was the wife of Nabal and is described as a clever and beautiful woman, in contrast to her husband that Scripture describes as churlish and mean. That mean-spiritedness causes Nabal to deny King David's request for provision and provokes David's wrath. Abigail, caught in the middle of these two flaring tempers, uses her gentle wisdom to quell a looming battle. After Nabal's death, David sends for her to become his wife, and she offers herself to him as a "servant," foreshadowing the "yes" Mary would one day offer the King for our salvation.

ABIGAIL

LECTIO

In one word, she is . . .

What is her role in Scripture?

☐ Wife ☐ Listener
☐ Mother ☐ Sinner
☐ Daughter ☐ Friend
☐ Teacher ☐ Other:_________

What does God ask of her?

MEDITATIO

What does she teach me about the nature of God?

What does she teach me about being a woman of God?

ORATIO

How does her story impact mine?

The first we hear of Abigail in Scripture is a description of her as "clever and beautiful," while her husband Nabal is described as "surly and mean" (1 Samuel 25:3). One has to wonder about a match between two such people. How long had Abigail been making amends for Nabal's offensive behavior? How long had her grace and kindness covered his lack thereof and saved her family? Abigail is a Hebrew name whose meaning is denoted as "gives joy," while Nabal means "senseless fool." It seems Abigail had spent many years trying to make joy prevail in a household where foolishness constantly put them at risk for destruction. Her encounter with David is one such incident.

David reaches out to Nabal asking for his help. He has helped Nabal by protecting and caring for Nabal's servants while they wandered the faraway fields in service to Nabal's household. David needs provisions for himself and his men to celebrate a feast and strengthen their weary bodies. But Nabal refuses to help and does so loudly and brashly. Abigail, hearing of the offense and fearing for her household, runs to the rescue, spurred on by her gracious disposition and quick-thinking mind. It is clear in her interactions with David that the beauty assigned to Abigail is not simply a physical beauty, but a beauty in the way she embodies her humanity, the way she lives her duty to respond to the needs of others and to help and protect them, even when it means protecting them from their own foolishness.

There are times I feel like I have spent a good portion of my life trying to protect others from their own foolish behavior and to mitigate the consequences of those behaviors when I cannot fully protect them. The difference in the outcome for me and our sister Abigail is knowing when I am protecting the people who deserve protection and when I am allowing a person to endure the consequences of a chosen behavior. Abigail ran out to ensure David's and his men's needs were met. First, I'm quite sure, to give him the respect that was due to a man of his rank, but also, it would seem, to act with the compassion and generosity that Nabal refused the troops. Abigail's actions also ensured the safety of the innocent members of her household who had done their proper duty. But Abigail could not and did not attempt to protect Nabal from the consequences of his lifelong choice to be callous and unresponsive to the needs of others.

When we use our wisdom to discern the proper course of action to generously serve, care for, and protect others, and focus that energy on the right people, we free ourselves from burdens to others whom we are not meant to protect or safeguard. In doing so, we are able to live fully generous lives. Self-preservation and limits are not a lack of compassion. They are a clever and beautiful use of our virtue that allow us the freedom to serve well and give ourselves fully in long-term service, because we do so from a healthy perspective that does not bind us or burden us in ways that are destructive to our spiritual well-being.

Abigail's wisdom shows me a new path forward in my relationships with others. I can be a protector and guardian. I can live with a compassionate and generous heart for others. And I can also safeguard myself and allow those people whose behavior I can't control to face the consequences of their behavior. There is freedom for me in that example. Many of us face the difficult circumstance of watching people we care about make decisions that negatively affect their lives. We have lived a constant chase to be one step ahead of their risks or to come behind to pick up the debris their actions leave, so we are well aware of how it exhausts and depletes our energy so that we have little left for the others in our lives who need us.

Wisdom, as exemplified by a holy woman like Abigail, invites us to let go of that burden and love from a place of true freedom and generosity. In doing so, we become a wellspring of love and beauty and kindness that can create a lifetime legacy of quiet but life-altering service. May we take to heart the lesson Abigail offers us and give ourselves fully to the task of laying down the burdens of others we are not meant to carry, so that we will have the strength to lift up those we are meant to bear.

Colleen Connell

GIFTED & GRACED

ON THE DIGNITY AND VOCATION OF WOMEN

This also explains the meaning of the "help" spoken of in Genesis 2:18-25: "I will make him a helper fit for him." The biblical context enables us to understand this in the sense that the woman must "help" the man—and in his turn he must help her—first of all by the very fact of their "being human persons." In a certain sense this enables man and woman to discover their humanity ever anew and to confirm its whole meaning. We can easily understand that—on this fundamental level—it is a question of a "help" on the part of both, and at the same time a mutual "help." To be human means to be called to interpersonal communion. The text of Genesis 2:18-25 shows that marriage is the first and, in a sense, the fundamental dimension of this call. But it is not the only one. The whole of human history unfolds within the context of this call. (7)

CONTEMPLATIO

What conversion of mind, heart, and life is the Lord asking of me?

ACTIO

Take a long, slow look at the people in your life. Which are the relationships that are right and good to protect and guard, and which are the ones that would be better let go?

Day Twenty-Eight

CONCLUSION

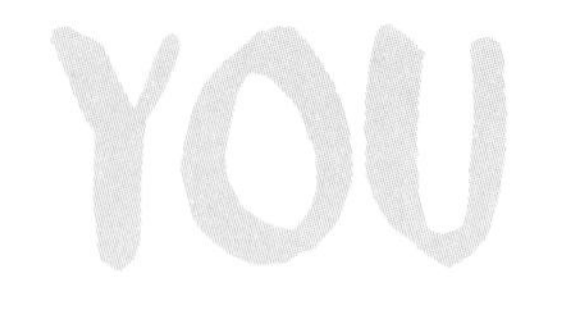

See what love the Father has given us,
that we should be called children of God;
and that is what we are.
The reason the world does not know us is
that it did not know him.
Beloved, we are God's children now;
what we will be has not
yet been revealed.
What we do know is this:
when he is revealed, we will be like him,
for we will see him as he is.
And all who have this hope in him
purify themselves, just as he is pure.

1 JOHN 3:1-3

FOR FURTHER STUDY

1 Corinthians 12:4-11; Ephesians 2:19-22

YOU
ARE
CALLED
TO BE
BLESSED.

Mine is a wide family. My children span in age from thirty years old to ten years old. Though I've been told they look as if they were all cut from a cookie cutter, they are a motley crew behind the similar countenances. There are four girls and five boys (five of each if you include my daughter-in-law). Mothering them has given me a front row seat to the diversity of human personalities. Each has his or her own quirks and talents and abilities and challenges. One thing is certain though.

They are all broken—even the littlest one. Life does that to a person.

We are wounded, all of us—all of them. There are days when they leave my house, and I want to call them back before they step off the front porch. I want to keep them here, safe and loved, as if somehow being home could restore to them the unscarred smoothness of a newly baptized baby's soul, the supple sweetness of a heart that has never been broken, not even a little bit. I want them to know every dream I dreamt for them when they were fresh from God and without the nicks and tarnish that living imparts.

I wish the world could see them through my eyes, that it could know the goodness in each of them that I do. I also wish that they could see themselves through my eyes, that they'd step off my front porch every day with the full assurance that they are loved beyond measure by a woman who would lay down her life for them. I wish they knew the boundless hope a mother feels for her children. I wish I could infuse in them the confidence and the comfort that come with knowing that they are unconditionally loved by another person on this planet.

But even if I could—even if they felt the full force of my human love—it would not be enough. Because I am wounded too, and I do not love perfectly. Further, I am not the author of their stories. I am only the woman God chose to open the book for them.

The only perfect love is the love God extends to us wholeheartedly. His is the fullness of love. He loves with a complete self-giving that is unfathomable to even the most devoted parent.

He calls to you with that love as you walk out the front door every day. You are his beloved daughter—dear and precious and good. You step into the day as a fellow citizen with God himself and as a member of his household (see Ephesians 2:19). His deepest desire is that you know this fact and that you live accordingly. Just like Sarah and Abigail and Ruth and Naomi and Martha and Mary, he nudges you off the porch and on your way, trying to remind you as you go that you are his and that he has a very intentional plan for you. You are a chosen and cherished person in his great story; he's crafted every single phrase with the greatest of care.

And as you walk into your day, people you pass pause and look twice. There, they see his unmistakable impression on you. You look like him; there is a family resemblance! In all the broken places, he makes you new again. The story he wants to write with you is a family story, and he is inextricably woven into it.

You are a child of God who walks with all the dignity of that supernatural status. You will be known by the way your story is written. And you coauthor the story with God himself by being a doer of the word (see James 1:22). His story come to life in your being is the story he intends for you. Together, we join our stories to those of the women of the Bible, to continue to impact the world as women touched and changed by God. It's a story of righteousness and reaching for holiness and loving one another as we are—a wide family whose members each bear a certain resemblance to one another and who also recognize God in the broken places of their lives.

Elizabeth Foss

GIFTED & GRACED

ON THE DIGNITY AND VOCATION OF WOMEN

The Church gives thanks for all the manifestations of the feminine "genius" which have appeared in the course of history, in the midst of all peoples and nations; she gives thanks for all the charisms which the Holy Spirit distributes to women in the history of the People of God, for all the victories which she owes to their faith, hope and charity: she gives thanks for all the fruits of feminine holiness.

The Church asks at the same time that these invaluable "manifestations of the Spirit" (cf. 1 Cor 12:4ff.), which with great generosity are poured forth upon the "daughters" of the eternal Jerusalem, may be attentively recognized and appreciated so that they may return for the common good of the Church and of humanity, especially in our times. Meditating on the biblical mystery of the "woman," the Church prays that in this mystery all women may discover themselves and their "supreme vocation." (31)

CONTEMPLATIO

What conversion of mind, heart, and life is the Lord asking of me?

ACTIO

You are a beloved child of God. Here, today, begins the rest of your story. For a moment, allow yourself to ponder that the story he intends for you is better than any you can imagine. How does it begin?

SELAH

Use this day for pause, prayer, praise, and rest.

Weekly Check-In

THE BEST TIME TO STUDY	A PLACE I FIND QUIET
______________________	______________________

AS I STUDY *CALL ME BLESSED*, I'M FEELING

○ *happy*	○ *anxious*	○ *annoyed*	○ *grateful*	○ ____________
○ *excited*	○ *upset*	○ *angry*	○ *confused*	○ ____________
○ *joyful*	○ *tired*	○ *sad*	○ *calm*	○ ____________

My heart is changing:

God is changing:

Scripture I can't shake:

A woman of God I want to reflect:

Women in my prayers:

Asking for Mary's intercession:

Grateful for:

Colleen Connell is a bringer-upper-of-boys and wannabe saint who packs a little Louisiana spice with her wherever she goes. She currently serves at-risk families in her job as a social worker in Fort Wayne, Indiana, and spends copious hours on football and soccer fields yelling more loudly than all the other moms. She finds joy in the word, the world, and the wild wonder of everyday life.

Katie Curtis grew up in Chicago but moved to the East Coast in high school, and now lives in Portsmouth, NH, with her giant Scottish husband and six kids (including one-year-old twin boys). A midwest girl at heart, she loves her neighbors, coffee, and conversations that get deep. When she isn't writing or cooking, she is driving her kids to sports or getting gummed on by babies. Her ideal day includes a writing session, a Rosary, a run, a dance party with her kids, and everyone home for a yummy dinner.

Micaela Darr is a California girl, born and raised, with brief stints in Mexico, Spain, and South Korea. She's extroverted by nature, but being a mom of seven kids has driven her to appreciate having quiet alone time too. Her husband, Kevin, is the best in the world, especially because he's exceedingly patient in regards to her harebrained schemes (see living in South Korea). Micaela is disorganized by nature but is also bound and determined to improve herself in that area and has done so with a modicum of success. She loves to read, watch good TV, and chat your ear off.

Elizabeth Foss is a morning person who relishes her time alone with the word as much as she loves the inevitable interruption by the first child to wake. There is something so hopeful about every new day! A wife, mother, and grandmother, she's happy curled up with a good book or tinkering with a turn of phrase. She alternates between giving up coffee and perfecting cold brew. Elizabeth would rather be outdoors than inside, and she especially loves long walks in the Virginia countryside that sometimes break into a run.

Kristin Foss is a self-taught artist, plant person, thrifter, minimalist wannabe, and ENFP (who appreciates intimate gatherings). She loves a good street taco second to a loaded poke bowl, but most nights she's at home sharing a homemade dinner with her family. She gravitates towards bright, vibrant colors, and everything feminine and joyful. She believes that home is a priceless place and that there are no rules to your heart's idea of aesthetics and beauty.

Katy Greiner thinks all mornings would be better if they started with the Dexys Midnight Runners' classic "Come On Eileen." Her favorite way to waste time is by consuming quality long-form journalism that provokes big thoughts and therefore good conversation. When she's not looking over her shoulder for the real adult in the room to take care of her high school freshmen, she's planning her next trip or craving Chick-fil-A. She loves a good sunset, talking over texting, tea over coffee, all kinds of music, and hearing God laugh.

Meg Hunter-Kilmer is a hobo missionary who lives out of her car and travels around the world giving talks and retreats; in her heart, though, she lives in a house surrounded by lilacs in a small town in the South and spends her afternoons on the front porch with a stack of Young Adult princess books and a plate full of pastries. That not being an option, she spends much of her time making small talk, listening to audiobooks, and hunting down unlocked churches where she can make a holy hour. She hates bananas with a burning passion and used to keep a guitar pick in her wallet just in case—despite the fact that she doesn't play guitar.

Mary Lenaburg relishes entertaining. Her door is always open and the coffee hot. When traveling to speak, she loves to explore the local candy shops looking for the perfect dark chocolate fudge (with nuts is best). Mary spends her free time reading the latest best-selling murder mystery and baking her famous chocolate chip cookies, ensuring that the kitchen cookie jar is always full. Mary and her husband have been happily married for thirty years, finding joy among the ashes, having lost their disabled daughter, Courtney, in 2014. They live in Northern Virginia with their grown son, Jonathan.

Rakhi McCormick is a wife and mother who works in parish communications part-time while trying to keep up with her husband, three young children, and a growing creative business in Metro Detroit. She is a first-generation Indian-American and a convert from Hinduism. Rakhi has a passion for sharing the encouraging good news of the gospel. When not chasing her children, you can find her writing, singing, dreaming of Italy, and making beautiful things, all with coffee in hand.

Allison McGinley recently moved to the Philly suburbs with her husband and two kids and is living her dream with a church, library, and diner within walking distance. She returned to her faith during college, and nothing has been the same ever since, in the best way. Writing is the way she processes life and discovers the beauty all around her, and she's been known to write in her closet in the middle of the night when the right words are suddenly found. She's happiest when taking photos of beautiful things, worshipping God through song, drinking a cup of coffee, or standing by the ocean.

For nearly a decade, some friends have had a desire to write and share devotions to go along with daily Scripture study. We've traded essays back and forth in various places, and we've grown in friendship with each other and the Lord. In spring 2017, the opportunity to widen our circle presented itself. We gathered a few more women, across generations, and wrote some small essays that would inspire us—and you— to daily take up the word and read it.

In printed journals that you can hold in your hands and touch with your pens, we collected our conversations with God. These volumes allow us to both commit at least a little time daily to honest conversation with God in his word and to dig more deeply and respond more carefully when we have the grace to do so.

We are Catholic women who hear and pray the word liturgically in our worship spaces but seek also to make Christ personal in our hearts and our homes. And we welcome our sisters from across denominations into our conversations at our website and on social media.

We know that the Bible is God's story for us. And we want to live in the center of that holy narrative every day. We want God's word to give us words for one another, a common language of love in him.

God's word endures—across the seasons of a woman's life, it is the constant. He is faithful every day. In every restless night, in every joyous celebration, in all the ordinary days in between, we can and do seek the voice of our Lord in his holy Scripture.

We take our name from the pages of St. Augustine's *Confessions*. Now a Doctor of the Church, Augustine was living a life of miserable debauchery when he was compelled by the Holy Spirit to take up his Bible and read it. His entire world changed in a moment of conversation with the word.

We believe that ours can too—on an ordinary day, in an ordinary living room or coffee shop or college dorm, to ordinary women. We pray it is so every single day.

Above All is a Lenten devotional journal that includes daily Scripture passages (set in context with enlightening historical notes to deepen your understanding), as well as devotional essays, room to journal, and space to organize your time. There is a simple prompt for the ancient prayer form of *Lectio Divina* each day, as well as a separate page for the fifth stage, *Actio*, where the reader is encouraged to examine her conscience and offer forgiveness to herself and to others. *Above All* is designed to help you reflect on all aspects of your life, particularly those that you may have pushed to the back burner. It's filled with tools to help you discover which areas need greater care and tending and is meant to inspire and motivate you to become your absolute truest self, so that come Easter, you can flourish as God intended.

Hosanna! is a Lenten walk with Jesus through the pages of the Book of Matthew. From his birth to his resurrection, readers are in step with the true God who is our salvation. Scripture, devotional reading, thoughtful journaling prompts, and inspiring art all come together to develop and deepen an intimate relationship between Jesus and you. This book will be available beginning February 2019.

Consider the Lilies: Maybe this is a difficult season in your life—you're overwhelmed by the burdens weighing you down, the crosses the Lord has asked you to carry. This study is for you. It is full of the consolations of the Holy Spirit; he is encouraging you to lament, to pour out your grief and your fears and your anger. Or maybe you're in a sweet spot. Life is really rather good right now. This study is for you too. It makes you a better friend to the woman next to you, to the growing child who aches, to the spouse who despairs. And it buries words into your heart so that they are there, waiting, when the rain begins to fall. Because it will fall.

Stories of Grace: Here you will find thirty-one days of Jesus' stories carefully collected for you. Along the way, we've provided meditation essays, journaling prompts, space for your notes and drawings, beautiful calligraphy pages, and prayers to draw you deeper into the parables Jesus told. Do you have eyes to see and ears to hear our Lord's stories of grace?

Ponder: An intimate encounter with the Rosary, this lovely volume integrates Bible study, journaling, and thoughtful daily action prompts. You will grow in your appreciation and understanding of the beautiful, traditional Rosary devotion, while deepening your love for Jesus in the Gospels.

Ponder for Kids: Created especially for children, this book contains Bible stories for every mystery of the Rosary. Full of interesting things to do, the journal is bursting with discussion questions, personal prayer prompts, puzzles, and coloring pages. There are also nature study pages to create a botanical rosary.

True Friend: Whether a woman is nineteen or forty-nine, friendship with other women can enrich our lives and can make us weep. How do we find friends who are kind and true? By becoming those friends ourselves. This beautiful book invites you to explore what God has to say about lasting friendships.

Flourish: To the people of Rome, the cultural center of the world at the time, St. Paul wrote the most comprehensive expression of the gospel. For us, the Book of Romans is a study of sin and guilt, loss and rescue. It is the essential gospel. An in-depth look at the entire Book of Romans, this study provides inspiration and structure to dig deeply into St. Paul's guidebook for the early Church—and for we who are the Church today.

All are available at amazon.com

She Reads Truth Bible. Nashville: Holman Bible Publishers, 2017.

The Didache Bible: With Commentaries Based on the Catechism of the Catholic Church. San Francisco: Ignatius Press, 2015.

The Navarre Bible: New Testament Expanded Edition. New York: Scepter Press, 2008.

Godden, Rumer. *In This House of Brede. Kindle edition.* New York: Open Lane Integrated Media, 2016.

Hahn, Scott, general editor. *Catholic Bible Dictionary.* New York: Doubleday Religion, 2009.

Hahn, Scott, editor, and Curtis Mitch, compiler. *Ignatius Catholic Study Bible: New Testament.* San Francisco: Ignatius Press, 2010.

Hardon, John, SJ. *Catholic Dictionary: A Modern and Updated Version of Modern Catholic Dictionary*. New York: Image, 2013.

John Paul II. *Mulieris Dignitatem* (On the Dignity and Vocation of Women). August 15, 1988. Accessed September 10, 2018. http://w2.vatican.va/content/john-paul-ii/en/apost_letters/1988/documents/hf_jp-ii_apl_19880815_mulieris-dignitatem.html_edn33.

---. General audience. Vatican website. April 10, 1996. Accessed September 9, 2018. https://w2.vatican.va/content/john-paul-ii/it/audiences/1996/documents/hf_jp-ii_aud_19960410.html.

---. General audience. Vatican website. May 28, 1997. Accessed September 11, 2018. http://w2.vatican.va/content/john-paul-ii/en/audiences/1997/documents/hf_jp-ii_aud_28051997.html.

---.General audience. EWTN website. April 10, 1996. Accessed September 1, 2018. https://www.ewtn.com/library/papaldoc/jp2bvm16.htm.

---. Speech at the Meeting with the World of Suffering Shrine at St. Lazarus. El Rincón, La Habana, Cuba, January 24, 1998. https://www.ewtn.com/cuba/sick.htm.

This book was published by The Word Among Us. Since 1981, The Word Among Us has been answering the call of the Second Vatican Council to help Catholic laypeople encounter Christ in the Scriptures.

The name of our company comes from the prologue to the Gospel of John and reflects the vision and purpose of all of our publications: to be an instrument of the Spirit, whose desire is to manifest Jesus' presence in and to the children of God. In this way, we hope to contribute to the Church's ongoing mission of proclaiming the gospel to the world so that all people would know the love and mercy of our Lord and grow more deeply in their faith as missionary disciples.

Our monthly devotional magazine, *The Word Among Us*, features meditations on the daily and Sunday Mass readings, and currently reaches more than one million Catholics in North America and another half million Catholics in one hundred countries around the world. Our book division, The Word Among Us Press, publishes numerous books, Bible studies, and pamphlets that help Catholics grow in their faith.

To learn more about who we are and what we publish, log on to our website at www.wau.org. There you will find a variety of Catholic resources that will help you grow in your faith.